Rediscovering Joy
How Connecting with Your Inner Child Can Enhance Your Adult Life

Ellie Bloom

Copyright © 2024 by Ellie Bloom

All rights reserved.

No portion of this book may be reproduced in any form without written permission from the publisher or author, except as permitted by U.S. copyright law.

Contents

1. Introduction — 1
2. Understanding the Inner Child — 9
3. The Lost Connection — 17
4. Signs of Disconnection — 24
5. The Journey Back — 35
6. Playfulness and Creativity — 45
7. Emotional Healing — 57
8. Overcoming Resistance — 64
9. Integrating the Inner Child in Adult Life — 73
10. Relationships and the Inner Child — 82
11. The Inner Child at Work — 89
12. A Society Reconnected — 98
13. Conclusion — 105
14. Appendices — 110

Chapter 1

Introduction
Embracing Your Inner Child

Let's embark on an enlightening journey into a fascinating and insightful realm of our being–the concept of the "inner child." This may evoke a sense of nostalgia, an inkling of whimsy, or perhaps induce a slight feeling of confusion. Allow yourself to delve into this exploration with an open mind, appreciating both its complexity and its simplicity. The concept of the inner child, often regarded as an abstract and mysterious psychological construct, holds far-reaching implications touching myriad aspects of adult happiness and emotional intelligence.

Embracing this ever-present, yet often neglected facet of your psyche, could unlock significant enhancements in self-understanding and emotional wellbeing. Below are some theories about the notion of the "inner child."

Inner Child Theories

- John Bradshaw, a pioneering figure in the field of self-help and recovery, made significant contributions to our understanding of the inner child theory. He proposed that acknowledging and nurturing this vulnerable facet of our personality is key to our emotional health and well-being.

- The experience of childlike spontaneity and joy experienced in adulthood is often attributed to the successful integration of the person's inner child. This state of balance, which many people struggle to achieve, can be a source of creativity, inspiration, and overall contentment.

- Therapeutic techniques such as guided imagery, art therapy, and journaling are often utilized to access, understand, and comfort the inner child. These are considered effective ways to process unresolved childhood emotions or trauma and are pursued under the guidance of a certified professional.

- Famed psychotherapist Virginia Satir, known for her work in family therapy, firmly believed in the power of healing the inner child in order to improve relationships and build self-esteem in adulthood.

- A variety of theories exist on the influence of the inner child on an adult's mental health. Psychoanalyst Alice Miller, for example, argued that repressed memories and emotions from childhood can manifest as depression, anxiety, or other mental health concerns in adulthood.

- Certain negative patterns in our lives, such as chronic stress or unhealthy relationships, can be traced back to unresolved issues from our childhood. Recognizing and addressing this "inner child" can help break these patterns and pave the way towards a healthier mental and emotional state.

- Swiss psychiatrist Charles Baudouin, a contemporary of Carl Jung, expanded upon the inner child concept with his 'Child Complex'. He posited that the residue of childhood experiences can result in fixed, recurring patterns of behavior, emotions, and thoughts in adulthood.

At the intense pace of modern life, we often lose touch with the vibrant, carefree part of ourselves that once marveled in the wonders of pure imagination and unadulterated joy. This is the part of us that psychologists often refer to as our 'inner child'. Claiming ignorance of this concept can ultimately lead us to a jaded adult life devoid of simple happiness and spontaneous mirth. Keeping your inner child lively and well-nurtured, therefore, can be a significant step toward enriching your adult life with these quintessentially childlike qualities.

"Embracing your inner child is not about becoming childish," states Dr. Lucia Capacchione, a prominent art therapist and nationally recognized workshop leader, "but rather about reconnecting with the childlike attributes of wonder, joy, spontaneity, and creativity."

Understanding and welcoming this inherent element within us could be the key to achieving true happiness and fulfillment. This book delves into the concept of this inner child and its irrefutable significance in fostering adult contentment. Reconnecting with your inner child can help in healing past traumas. Many therapeutic approaches, such as Gestalt therapy, use techniques to help adults address unresolved childhood issues.

Engaging with your inner child can help in personal growth. It can lead to self-discovery and a better understanding of one's self, which are key components of personal development.

One potential barrier to unlocking one's inner child is societal expectations. Adults are often expected to behave in a certain way, conforming to societal norms and standards. This can stifle the freedom and spontaneity associated with our inner child, making it difficult to tap into this aspect of ourselves.

Another barrier is the fear of vulnerability. Embracing the inner child often means opening up to emotions and experiences that we have learned to suppress or ignore as adults. This can feel risky or uncomfortable, preventing us from fully engaging with our inner child.

Personal trauma or negative childhood experiences can also act as barriers. If an individual's childhood was marked by distressing events or circumstances, they may associate their inner child with these negative experiences, making it challenging to embrace this part of themselves.

Furthermore, the pressure to be productive and successful can also hinder us from unlocking our inner child. The inner child represents playfulness, creativity, and spontaneity, which are often devalued in favor of productivity and achievement in our adult lives.

Lastly, a lack of self-awareness can be a significant barrier. Without a deep understanding of ourselves, including our desires, fears, and emotional responses, it can be difficult to connect with our inner child. This requires introspection and self-reflection, which many people may struggle with or avoid. Embracing your inner child begins with self-awareness. This involves recognizing and acknowledging the existence of your inner child. This part of you is the essence of your first experiences and emotions. It's the source of your capacity for joy, wonder, and creativity. By acknowledging this part of you, you start the journey of embracing your inner child.

A study published in the Journal of Personality and Social Psychology published a study reporting that adults who regularly engage in playful activities, a characteristic often associated with the inner child, have higher levels of happiness and well-being. The researchers suggested that maintaining a sense of playfulness and curiosity, traits commonly associated with childhood, can contribute to a more joyful and satisfying adult life.

"The things which the child loves remain in the domain of the heart until old age. The most beautiful thing in life is that our souls remain over the places where we once enjoyed ourselves"

- Kahlil Gibran

Embracing the inner child can significantly contribute to adult happiness by allowing individuals to reconnect with their innate sense of curiosity and wonder. The inner child represents the core of a person's inherited potentialities, which include their capacity for joy, wonder, and creativity. By embracing this aspect of themselves, adults can reignite these qualities, leading to a more fulfilling and joyful life.

Stories of adults who have successfully reconnected with their inner child

Often as adults, we lose touch with the spontaneity and make-belief of our childhoods. However, embracing your "inner child" can be a key to finding happiness in adulthood. Let's take a closer look at the concept of the inner child and examine a case study to demonstrate its significance.

The term "inner child" refers to an individual's child-like aspect. It includes everything we learned and experienced as children before puberty. The feelings, experiences, and awareness of our inner child continue to influence our actions and decisions in adulthood.

A riveting case study that underlines this notion is that of John, a 50-year-old man. John, a successful businessman, felt a profound sense of dissatisfaction despite his financial success and seemingly perfect family life. He found his days monotonous, his interactions unfulfilling, and his life devoid of joy. Things took a turn when he was introduced to the concept of the inner child, during a personal development seminar.

During one of the sessions, John was asked to recall his happiest childhood memories and activities that used to bring him joy. He remembered his affinity for exploring the outdoors, picking up unique rocks and stones, and his love for painting. It was a realization for John–these were activities his 'inner child' loved, but he had abandoned with time, aligning his pursuits with societal notions of success and adulthood.

"There was a transformation in John when he started embracing his inner child. You could see a noticeable change in his demeanor, mood, and overall happiness," recalls Susan, John's life coach.

As part of his journey to embrace his inner child, John incorporated significant changes in his lifestyle. He started dedicating time to painting every week, took his family on nature explorations every month, and even started collecting rocks again. These simple changes, attuned with his inner child's interests, helped John rediscover the joy and happiness that was missing from his life. He reported feeling more content, happier, and more engaged in his daily activities than ever before.

To conclude, listening to your inner child and reincorporating elements of your childhood that brought you joy, could be instrumental in finding long-term happiness and satisfaction in adult life. This approach does not dismiss the responsibilities that come with adulthood but argues for a balanced life where joy, curiosity, and spontaneity have a place alongside duty and responsibility.

How Can Embracing Your Inner Child Improve Your Life?

- Authenticity: The inner child is a reflection of our true self, untouched by societal norms. When we embrace our inner child, we embrace our authenticity and core beliefs.

- Creativity Boost: Reconnecting with our inner child can spark creativity and innovation. The inner child is intrinsically curious and open to new experiences, which can benefit several areas of adult life, notably at work.

- Stress Reduction: Playing, daydreaming, and other child-like activities can help mitigate adult stress. Engaging in such activities offers a unique form of mental relaxation, which is essential for overall well-being.

- Improved Relationships: Embracing your inner child allows for more open and honest communication. This transparent interaction can lead to deeper and more meaningful relationships with loved ones.

- Self-awareness: Our inner child can inform us of unresolved issues and unmet needs. Acknowledging these can lead to a deeper understanding of one's self and potential personal growth.

- Evidence: Psychologists like Carl Jung and Eric Berne vouched for the existence of the inner child within our psyche, highlighting its influence on our daily lives.

- Relevance: Regardless of age or life stage, everyone has an inner child that embodies their early experiences and emotions. It remains a part of us throughout our lives and influences our responses to various situations.

Chapter 2

Understanding the Inner Child

Definition and Psychological Background of the Inner Child

The concept of the inner child has its roots in psychoanalytic theory. Carl Jung, a Swiss psychiatrist and psychoanalyst, was one of the first to propose the idea. He referred to it as the 'divine child' and believed it represented our true self, which is both vulnerable and powerful. The 'inner child' is a psychological concept that refers to an individual's childlike aspect, including everything one learned or experienced as a child before puberty. It is a semi-independent entity subordinate to the waking conscious mind. It embodies qualities like innocence, creativity, curiosity, joy, and sensitivity.

Jung's concept of the inner child, or 'divine child', is closely related to his theory of archetypes. Archetypes are universal, inborn models of people, behaviors, or personalities that play a role in influencing human behavior. The inner child is one such archetype.

Psychotherapist John Bradshaw further popularized the concept of the inner child in the late 20th century. He argued that many adults are unconsciously driven by the fears, anger, and joys of their childhood. He suggested that acknowledging and healing the inner child can lead to a resolution of adult emotional problems.

Bradshaw's work highlighted the importance of the inner child in understanding and treating a variety of mental health issues. He believed that unresolved childhood experiences could manifest as anxiety, depression, or other psychological distress in adulthood.

Today, the inner child concept is widely used in therapeutic settings. Therapists often encourage clients to communicate with, care for, and 're-parent' their inner child as a way to heal from past traumas and achieve emotional well-being. Inner child therapy is a form of psychotherapy that focuses on resolving adult issues that stem from unresolved childhood experiences. It's based on the concept that we all have an 'inner child' - a part of our psyche that remains childlike and carries the innocence, curiosity, and vulnerability of our younger selves.

Inner child therapy aims to help individuals reconnect with this often neglected or suppressed part of themselves. By doing so, it can address problems such as low self-esteem, problematic behaviors, and relationship issues that may be rooted in childhood trauma or neglect.

The process involves exploring past experiences and emotions that may have been ignored or suppressed. This can be achieved through various techniques such as guided imagery, journaling, art therapy, and role-playing. The goal is to help the individual understand and heal their inner child, leading to a more balanced and fulfilled adult life.

Therapies/Methods for Inner Child Work

The inner child is a psychological construct that represents the child-like aspects of a person's psyche. It has roots in psychoanalytic theory and is used in therapy to help adults resolve emotional issues and achieve happiness. The inner child represents the part of your personality that still reacts and feels like a child. This component of your psyche holds your innocence, creativity, awe, and wonder. It's also the source of your deepest emotional needs, which include the need for love, safety, and validation.

The need for love is perhaps the most fundamental need of the inner child. This love can come from various sources, such as self-love, love from family and friends, or romantic love. The inner child seeks to feel loved and cherished, and when this need is unmet, it can lead to feelings of loneliness, insecurity, and low self-esteem.

The inner child also craves safety and security. This need is rooted in our early childhood experiences, where our survival depended on the protection of our caregivers. As adults, we continue to seek environments and relationships that make us feel safe and secure. When this need is not met, it can result in anxiety, fear, and a lack of trust in others.

Validation is another crucial need of the inner child. This involves recognition and acceptance of one's feelings, thoughts, and experiences. When our inner child feels heard and understood, it fosters self-esteem and a sense of worthiness. However, when this need is unfulfilled, it can lead to feelings of invisibility, insignificance, and a lack of self-confidence.

Beyond these needs, the inner child also seeks to express itself. This can be through creative activities such as art, music, or dance, or through play and exploration. The inner child is naturally curious and loves to learn and discover new things. When we allow our inner child to express itself, we can experience joy, wonder, and a sense of fulfillment.

However, it's important to note that the inner child can also express negative emotions such as anger, sadness, or fear. These emotions are often a response to unmet needs or past traumas. Acknowledging and addressing these feelings is a crucial part of healing and nurturing the inner child.

"Nurturing the needs and expressions of the inner child is crucial, as these reflect our deepest desires and fundamental emotional responses. These are the roots from where our personality grows, and therefore, these aspects require attentive cultivation." - Dr. Carl Rogers, known for his work on humanistic psychology

Recognizing these needs, as well as allowing these expressions of our inner child, becomes a major aspect in our journey towards self-evolution and the pursuit of genuine happiness.

Understanding and meeting the needs of the inner child, as well as allowing its expression, can lead to a happier and more fulfilled adult life. It encourages self-love, reduces anxiety, and promotes a sense of worthiness and joy.

Examples of Needs and Expressions of Inner Child

1. Physical and Emotional Safety: The inner child craves a sense

of security. It desires a safe, nurturing environment where it can grow and express itself freely and without fear of harm or rejection.

2. Love and Affection: The need for love and connection is integral to the inner child. It seeks constant reassurance that it is loved, cherished, and accepted unconditionally.

3. Attention and Validation: As a form of external approval, the inner child yearns for acknowledgment and validation of its feelings, thoughts, and achievements.

4. Expression of Emotions: The inner child is expressive and wants its feelings–be they joy, sadness, anger, or fear - to be recognized and understood.

5. Freedom to Explore: The inner child is curious and adventurous. It seeks the liberty to explore the world, experiment with new things, make its own mistakes and learn from them.

Case Studies

The concept of the inner child has been explored in various case studies, each highlighting the importance of embracing this aspect of ourselves for overall happiness. One notable study conducted by psychologist Dr. Lucia Capacchione involved adults who were struggling with depression and anxiety. Through a series of therapy sessions, these individuals were encouraged to reconnect with their inner child, often through creative activities like drawing or writing. The results showed a significant improvement in their mental health, with many reporting increased levels of joy and contentment.

Dr. Lucia Capacchione is a renowned art therapist, artist, and author who has contributed significantly to the field of expressive arts therapy. She holds a Ph.D. in psychology and is recognized for her pioneering work in using art therapy for self-discovery and healing.

Dr. Capacchione's work is centered around the concept of the 'inner child', a psychological construct that represents an individual's original or true self. She believes that by reconnecting with this inner child, adults can unlock a sense of joy, creativity, and authenticity that contributes to overall happiness and well-being.

Her methodology involves using creative journaling and drawing exercises to help individuals access and express their inner child. These exercises are designed to bypass the logical, analytical mind and tap into the subconscious, where the inner child resides.

Her work has been influential in various fields, including psychology, counseling, art therapy, and personal growth. Many therapists and coaches use her methods to help clients overcome emotional trauma, improve self-esteem, and enhance personal and professional creativity.

Dr. Capacchione's approach to embracing the inner child aligns with the growing recognition of the importance of emotional health and self-expression in adult happiness. By helping individuals reconnect with their inner child, she provides a pathway to a more joyful, authentic life.

Another case study worth mentioning is the work of Dr. Margaret Paul, a psychologist who specializes in inner bonding therapy. She worked with a group of adults who had experienced childhood trauma. By helping them to reconnect with their inner child, she was able to guide them toward healing and self-love. Over time, these individuals reported a decrease in their trauma-related symptoms and an increase in their overall happiness.

Another interesting case study was conducted by Dr. Stephen Diamond, a clinical and forensic psychologist. He worked with adults who were struggling with anger management issues. By helping them to understand and embrace their inner child, he was able to help them express their anger in healthier ways. This not only improved their relationships but also their personal happiness.

Lastly, a study by Dr. Charles Whitfield delved into the concept of the inner child in relation to addiction. He found that many adults who struggle with addiction have unresolved issues from their childhood that they've been unable to face. By helping them to reconnect with their inner child, he was able to guide them toward understanding and healing these issues. As a result, many of these individuals were able to overcome their addictions and improve their overall quality of life.

Carl Jung, a Swiss psychiatrist and psychoanalyst, was one of the pioneers in exploring the concept of the 'inner child'. He referred to it as the 'Divine Child' archetype, which represents the original, untouched essence of a person. This archetype is characterized by innocence, vulnerability, and a sense of wonder.

According to Jung, embracing the inner child can lead to a more fulfilling adult life. He argued that our adult personality is largely influenced by the experiences of our childhood. By reconnecting with our inner child, we can heal past wounds, understand our true desires, and regain a sense of joy and curiosity.

Jung's concept of the inner child is not about becoming childish, but rather about acknowledging and integrating the childlike aspects of our personality into our adult selves. This includes qualities like spontaneity, creativity, playfulness, and the ability to live in the moment.

Overall, Carl Jung's concept of the inner child suggests that our happiness and fulfillment as adults are deeply linked to our ability to reconnect with and embrace the childlike aspects of our personality. By doing so, we can unlock a sense of joy, wonder, and authenticity that can enrich our lives.

Chapter 3

The Lost Connection

How and Why We Lose Touch with Our Inner Child

"Every child is an artist, the problem is staying an artist when you grow up."

- Pablo Picasso

The brain of a child is incredibly adaptable and flexible. This neuroplasticity allows children to learn new skills, languages, and behaviors with relative ease. Embracing this aspect of your inner child can lead to lifelong learning and adaptability.

Children's brains are also more open to new experiences and ideas. This openness can lead to creativity and innovation in adulthood. By embracing your inner child, you can tap into this openness and bring more creativity and innovation into your life.

Subsequently, Children are naturally curious and eager to explore the world around them. This curiosity fuels their learning and growth. As adults, embracing this curiosity can lead to personal and professional growth, as well as a deeper understanding of the world. They are also more likely to express their emotions openly and honestly. This emotional honesty can lead to healthier relationships and a greater sense of well being. By embracing your inner child, you can learn to express your emotions more openly and honestly, and find delight in simple pleasures and are often filled with awe at the beauty of the world.

The Impact of Societal Expectations On The Inner Child

As we grow older, however, societal expectations and pressures often lead us to lose touch with our inner child. We are taught to prioritize logic and reason over imagination and playfulness, which can cause us to suppress our inner child.

Children are often more present and engaged in the moment than adults. This ability to be fully present can lead to greater enjoyment of life's experiences. Embracing this aspect of your inner child can help you to live more fully in the moment and find joy in everyday experiences.

Another reason we lose touch with our inner child is the fear of judgment or ridicule. As children, we are naturally uninhibited and expressive. However, as we grow older, we become more aware of societal norms and expectations. This can lead to self-censorship and the suppression of our childlike qualities in order to fit in or avoid criticism.

Life experiences and traumas can also cause us to disconnect from our inner child. Painful experiences can lead us to build emotional walls and adopt coping mechanisms that distance us from our true selves. It can lead to emotional, psychological, and even physical issues. These traumas can cause the inner child to become 'stuck' at the age at which the trauma occurred, leading to patterns of behavior, emotional responses, and beliefs that are characteristic of that developmental stage.

Trauma can cause the inner child to feel unsafe, leading to a variety of defense mechanisms such as dissociation, repression, or hyper-vigilance. These defense mechanisms can persist into adulthood, affecting relationships, self-esteem, and overall mental health, but embracing your inner child in the face of trauma exercises self-compassion. It's about acknowledging the past, living in the present, and looking forward to a future where the inner child is not just surviving, but thriving.

Inner child therapy, also known as inner child work, is a therapeutic approach that addresses traumatic experiences from childhood that may still be affecting an individual's emotional health in adulthood. Trauma experienced during childhood can have long-lasting effects on an individual's mental and emotional health. Inner child therapy aims to address and heal these wounds by reconnecting with the inner child and reprocessing the traumatic experiences.

Expert Insights

During inner child therapy, the therapist guides the individual to recall and revisit traumatic childhood experiences. The goal is not to relive the trauma but to understand and reinterpret it from an adult perspective. This process can help the individual to release pent-up emotions, develop self-compassion, and break destructive patterns of behavior.

Techniques used in inner child therapy can include guided imagery, journaling, art therapy, and role-play. These methods help the individual to access their inner child, express their feelings, and create a dialogue between their adult self and their inner child. This dialogue can help to resolve unresolved issues and foster a healthier relationship with the self.

Inner child therapy can be a powerful tool for personal growth and healing. By embracing and nurturing our inner child, we can release old wounds, cultivate self-love, and unlock greater joy and happiness in our adult lives. However, it's important to note that this therapy should be conducted under the guidance of a trained professional, as revisiting childhood trauma can be emotionally challenging.

One of the most common techniques used in inner child therapy is dialogue writing. This involves writing a conversation between the adult self and the inner child. The adult self asks questions and provides reassurance, while the inner child expresses feelings and concerns. This technique helps to establish a connection between the adult self and the inner child, enabling the individual to address unresolved issues.

Guided imagery is another effective technique used in inner child therapy. The therapist guides the individual through a series of visualizations designed to evoke memories of childhood. This can help the individual to access and understand emotions associated with these memories.

Reparenting is a crucial component of inner child therapy. This involves the adult self 'parenting' the inner child in a way that the individual may not have experienced in their actual childhood. This can include providing the inner child with validation, comfort, and protection.

Art therapy can also be used as a part of inner child therapy. This technique allows individuals to express their feelings and experiences in a non-verbal way through drawing, painting, or other forms of artistic expression. This can be particularly helpful for those who find it difficult to articulate their feelings verbally.

Play therapy is another technique that can be used in inner child therapy. This involves engaging in play as a way to reconnect with the inner child. Play therapy can help individuals to express emotions, explore repressed memories, and develop problem-solving skills.

Finally, mindfulness and meditation can also be incorporated into inner child therapy. These techniques can help individuals to stay present and focused during the therapy process, and can also assist in managing any difficult emotions that may arise. The inner child represents playfulness, creativity, and spontaneity, which are often devalued in favor of productivity and achievement in our adult lives.

"Man is most nearly himself when he achieves the seriousness of a child at play."

- Heraclitus

Embracing your inner child in the context of trauma recovery means acknowledging and addressing the pain, trauma, or neglect that this part of you has experienced. It involves learning to nurture and care for your inner child, providing the love, support, and validation that may have been lacking in your childhood. Embracing your inner child can lead to profound personal growth. This process allows you to reconnect with some of the core aspects of your personality, perhaps forgotten over time. It can help you rediscover your natural curiosity, creativity, and the ability to live in the moment.

Embracing your inner child can lead to increased joy and vitality in life. Children are naturally joyful, energetic, and enthusiastic. By reconnecting with these qualities, you can bring more positivity and energy into your adult life.

How Can Embracing My Inner Child Improve My Life?

- Authenticity: The inner child is a reflection of our true self, untouched by societal norms. When we embrace our inner child, we embrace our authenticity and core beliefs.

- Creativity Boost: Reconnecting with our inner child can spark creativity and innovation. The inner child is intrinsically curious and open to new experiences, which can benefit several areas of adult life, notably at work.

- Stress Reduction: Playing, daydreaming, and other child-like activities can help mitigate adult stress. Engaging in such activities offers a unique form of mental relaxation, which is essential for overall well-being.

- Improved Relationships: Embracing your inner child allows for more open and honest communication. This transparent interaction can lead to deeper and more meaningful relationships with loved ones.

- Self-awareness: Our inner child can inform us of unresolved issues and unmet needs. Acknowledging these can lead to a deeper understanding of one's self and potential personal growth.

- Evidence: Psychologists like Carl Jung and Eric Berne vouched for the existence of the inner child within our psyche, highlighting its influence on our daily lives.

- Relevance: Regardless of age or life stage, everyone has an inner child that embodies their early experiences and emotions. It remains a part of us throughout our lives and influences our responses to various situations.

Chapter 4

Signs of Disconnection

Recognizing the symptoms of a neglected inner child in adulthood

The concept of the 'neglected inner child' refers to the psychological perspective that unresolved childhood experiences, emotions, and traumas can continue to impact an individual's behavior, emotional health, and happiness in adulthood. This is often characterized by feelings of emptiness, low self-esteem, and a lack of fulfillment.

The neglected inner child is a metaphorical representation of the emotional needs that were not adequately met during one's childhood. This could be due to various reasons such as parental neglect, abuse, or even the lack of emotional support and understanding from caregivers. These unmet needs can manifest in adulthood as emotional dysregulation, difficulties in relationships, and struggles with self-care.

When the inner child is neglected, adults may find themselves stuck in harmful patterns of behavior that were developed as coping mechanisms during their childhood. These behaviors can include self-sabotage, avoidance of intimacy, or an excessive need for approval from others. They may also struggle with feelings of inadequacy, fear of abandonment, or a deep-seated belief that they are undeserving of love and happiness.

The neglected inner child in adulthood often manifests as chronic dissatisfaction. Despite having achieved societal markers of success, such as a good job or a stable relationship, individuals may still feel a persistent sense of emptiness or unfulfillment. This could be a sign that the emotional needs of their inner child were not met during their formative years.

"You can be childlike without being childish. A child always wants to have fun. Ask yourself, 'Am I having fun?'"

- Christopher Meloni

Another symptom of a neglected inner child is a pervasive sense of guilt or shame. Adults may find themselves constantly feeling as though they are not good enough, or that they have to hide their true selves to be accepted. This often stems from childhood experiences where their emotions, needs, or identities were invalidated or dismissed.

Individuals with a neglected inner child may also struggle with setting and maintaining boundaries. They may find it difficult to say no to others, often at the expense of their own well-being. This is often a result of a childhood where their boundaries were not respected, leading them to believe that their needs and feelings are less important than those of others.

Addiction and other compulsive behaviors can also be indicative of a neglected inner child (see Chapter 2 for more on addiction and the inner child). These behaviors are often coping mechanisms for unprocessed emotional pain from childhood. Individuals may turn to substances, food, work, or other distractions to numb or avoid their feelings.

Difficulty in forming and maintaining healthy relationships is another sign of a neglected inner child. Individuals may find themselves drawn to toxic relationships, or they may struggle with trust and intimacy. This can stem from early experiences of neglect, abuse, or inconsistent care.

A neglected inner child can manifest as physical symptoms. Chronic stress, anxiety, and depression can lead to a range of physical health issues, including headaches, digestive problems, and sleep disorders. These symptoms are often the body's way of signaling unmet emotional needs.

Recognizing symptoms of a neglected inner child in adulthood often involves identifying patterns of behavior, emotional responses, and thought processes that may be rooted in childhood experiences. One of the most common signs is chronic anxiety. This can manifest as a constant feeling of worry or unease, often without a clear cause. It's as if the person is always waiting for something bad to happen, a pattern that may have originated in an unstable or unpredictable childhood environment.

Another symptom is a deep-seated fear of abandonment. Adults who have neglected their inner child may be hypersensitive to rejection and may go to great lengths to avoid being alone or feeling unwanted. This can lead to clingy behavior in relationships and a tendency to stay in unhealthy situations out of fear of being left alone.

Difficulty setting boundaries is another sign of a neglected inner child. This can manifest as a tendency to let others take advantage of them, an inability to say no, or a pattern of self-sacrifice to the point of self-neglect. This often stems from a childhood where the person's needs and feelings were not respected or acknowledged.

Adults with a neglected inner child may also struggle with chronic feelings of emptiness or unfulfillment. They may have a hard time finding joy or satisfaction in life, often feeling as though something is missing. This can be a result of not having their emotional needs met in childhood, leading to a lifelong search for something to fill the void.

Finally, a neglected inner child can lead to a harsh inner critic. Adults may constantly judge and criticize themselves, often to a debilitating degree. They may struggle with feelings of worthlessness and a persistent belief that they are not good enough. This harsh self-judgment can stem from a childhood where they were criticized, belittled, or made to feel inadequate.

Recognizing these symptoms is the first step towards healing the neglected inner child. By acknowledging these patterns and understanding their roots in childhood experiences, adults can begin to nurture their inner child, leading to greater self-acceptance, emotional healing, and ultimately, a happier and more fulfilling adult life.

How to Check In with Your Inner Child

Self-assessment begins with recognizing and understanding your emotional reactions. If you find yourself overreacting to situations, it may be your inner child responding. These reactions often stem from unresolved childhood experiences or traumas.

To effectively embrace your inner child, you must acknowledge these instinctive emotional responses, objectively evaluate their roots, and gradually find healthy methods to cope with them. The cognitive process of introspection often assists in this pursuit. Note down certain situations where you feel your behavior deviated from your normal responses, then trace it back to any unresolved incident in your past. This might help you discern the triggers, casting light on the deep-seated emotions your inner child is battling.

As you contemplate on this journey of self-discovery, finding a connection with your inner child becomes imperative—both for personal growth and overall well-being. Here are a few introspective questions that can assist you in assessing your connection with your inner child. Keep in mind, that honesty is key to fruitful self-assessment.

Inner Child Self-assessment

- Do you feel energized by creative activities? The inner child thrives on creativity. If you're genuinely drawn to artistic activities like painting, writing, or just day-dreaming, this could be a sign of a strong connection with your inner child.

- Can you freely express your emotions? Children are naturally expressive with their feelings. If you can genuinely feel and express emotions—both positive and negative—that might mean your inner child is alive and active.

- Do you retain a sense of wonder about the world? Children are natural explorers. They gaze at the world with wide-eyed wonder. If you find yourself completely captivated by the simple things around you, it suggests a robust connection to your inner child.

- Are you comfortable with play? Playfulness is a trademark of childhood. If you can lose yourself in fun and playful activities, without feeling self-conscious, it may indicate a healthy bond with your inner child.

- Can you forgive easily? Another wonderful quality of children is their readiness to forgive. If you too can let go of grudges quickly, your inner child appears to be in close sync with your adult self.

Bear in mind that these questions serve merely as a guide — understanding one's inner child is a highly individual process. Most importantly, embrace any vulnerabilities you uncover along the way. After all, it's often within these areas of vulnerability that we find our greatest room for growth.

Initiating the journey towards embracing your inner child requires conscious effort and contemplation. Comprehending your buried emotions from childhood can illuminate aspects of your adult behavior, which may be instrumental in maximizing your potential for happiness and fulfillment. The process, while deeply personal, can be guided by a few universal steps:

Firstly, engage in reflection. Look back on your childhood experiences, both joyous and challenging. How did you feel during these times and why? What activities made you feel truly alive? What fears held you back? This reflective exercise serves not only to understand your past but also to uncover aspects of your personality that may have been buried beneath the layers of adulthood.

Secondly, permit yourself to feel your emotions – all of them. If you uncover old wounds or relive past fears, allow these feelings to flow through you as it is a significant part of the healing process. Neglecting or suppressing these emotions only furthers their ascendancy over your current state of happiness. Remember, it's completely natural and healthy to feel a full spectrum of emotions.

Thirdly, cultivate practices that fuel your sense of playfulness, creativity and spontaneity–innate attributes of the child within. This could involve breathing new life into old hobbies or discovering new ones, embracing a more exploratory curiosity about the world, or simply allowing yourself the freedom to laugh and play without judgment or restriction.

Lastly, practice compassion towards yourself. Embracing your inner child also means accepting yourself in entirety, with all your strengths, weaknesses, and vulnerabilities. It implies nurturing yourself with love and kindness and forgiving yourself for past mistakes. It is only once you truly accept yourself that you can embark upon a journey steeped in genuine joy and contentment.

Undertaking these steps will equip you with a heightened understanding of your inner child, a crucial step towards liberating happiness and fulfillment in your adult life. Remember, the path of inner exploration is a continually unfolding journey, not a one-time task to be completed and shelved. As you navigate through this exploration, you will not only perceive the world through a richer, more vivid lens, but also embody a more authentic, joy-filled version of yourself.

Our inner child is, essentially, an amalgam of playfulness, curiosity, emotional vulnerability, creativity, and innocence, accounts for our overall temperament and perspective as adults. To understand and reconnect with these facets translates into embracing our inner child and ultimately, leading a more enriched, happier adult life. So, how do we reconnect to a neglected inner child?

Reflections from Therapists and Psychologists

Renowned therapists and psychologists often emphasize the importance and role of the inner child in adult mental health. They recognize the inner child as an integral part of our adult selves, serving as a reflection of the child we once were. It's defined as a sub-personality or secondary persona within the adult personality, often manifested through our behaviors, attitudes, and emotional responses that seem to echo our childhood.

According to Dr. Lucia Capacchione, a therapist known for her work with the inner child concept, "When we ignore and suppress the voice of our inner child, we block access to a key part of our emotional and psychological makeup." She believes that acknowledging and nurturing our inner child can lead to a greater sense of fulfillment and psychological health.

Therapists argue that the experiences we have as children–both positive and negative–leave profound imprints on our adult selves. Recognizing and addressing these influences can be an enriching process. A primal instance can be, if as a child, your emotional needs were often overlooked, you might struggle with self-expression as an adult. Or if you faced frequent criticism growing up, you might wrestle with self-esteem issues in adulthood.

Engaging with your inner child, as therapists suggest, can offer deep insights into these unconscious influences. One effective method is through inner child therapy or re-parenting. This involves establishing a sort of dialogue with your inner child, typically facilitated by a trained therapist. It is a strategy aimed at resolving childhood experiences and feelings that have unconsciously shaped your adult life.

The overall consensus within the therapy community is that learning to accept, nurture, and express your inner child can be a game-changer for many adults struggling with their mental health. Embracing your inner child isn't about reverting to immaturity, rather it's about recognizing and processing the experiences that have molded your adult self.

Let's explore a case study to further illustrate how embracing your inner child can bring about transformative change. We turn to Jane, a client of renowned inner child therapist Dr. Alice Woods. Jane, a successful corporate executive, had always struggled with a sense of emotional disconnection and dissatisfaction despite her professional achievements.

Through her sessions with Dr. Woods, Jane began the journey of reconnecting to her inner child that she had pushed aside and dismissed due to societal influences and her pursuit of a traditional notion of success. Dr. Woods used a variety of therapeutic interventions, including guided imagery, to help Jane visualize and engage with her inner child in a safe, nurturing space.

The role-play exercises were particularly impactful, enabling Jane to give her inner child a voice and to establish a nurturing dialogue. This was not always an easy process. Embracing her inner child meant acknowledging unprocessed emotions from her childhood, including fear, sadness, and feelings of unimportance. Revisiting these emotions was challenging but necessary for Jane's emotional healing.

The sessions provided profound insight for Jane, she was able to understand how her adult life, shaped by various societal and personal influences, had caused her to lose touch with her inner child. Recognizing this disconnect was a crucial step toward rectifying it.

As Jane continued her therapeutic journey, she noticed incremental changes in her sense of self and happiness. She found herself more in touch with her inner joy, more attuned to her emotional needs, and more compassionate towards herself. She also reported improved relationships with colleagues, friends, and family, signifying an expansive positive impact of the process.

This case study not just underscores the power of inner child therapy, but also stands as a testament to the transformative potential of embracing the inner child. The journey, while challenging, can lead to an enriched and authentic state of happiness, as evidenced in Jane's life transformation.

Ultimately, embracing your inner child is a daring journey of self-discovery and healing. It asks you to reexamine past hurts, old habits, and engrained defenses, diving deep into the murky waters of your earliest memories. Here, you engage with your unexpressed emotions, forgotten fantasies, and squashed curiosities, shedding light on, and reconciling with the whimsical, innocent soul that once shaped your approach to life. The work is, undoubtedly, arduous and emotionally taxing; yet, the potential rewards are enormous.

True happiness is not perpetual positivity or an unwavering smile. It's the acceptance and love for your complete self, including the small child hidden within your adult shell. As proven through numerous case studies like Jane's, nurturing your inner child can be a powerful catalyst for transformation, leading to authentic happiness, renewed creativity, sharp intuition, and a pure sense of natural happiness. Remember, it's never too late to heal your inner child—and in doing so, reshape the narrative of your life.

Chapter 5

The Journey Back

Steps to Reconnect with The Inner Child

The first step to reconnecting with your inner child is self-reflection. This involves taking time to think about your childhood experiences, both positive and negative. Reflect on what made you happy, what made you sad, and what made you feel loved. This process can help you identify the aspects of your childhood that have shaped your adult self.

Next, engage in activities that you enjoyed as a child. This could be anything from drawing, painting, playing a musical instrument, or even playing a sport. These activities can help you tap into the joy and freedom that you experienced as a child and can help you reconnect with your inner child.

Another important step is to practice mindfulness. This involves being present in the moment, and not worrying about the past or the future. Mindfulness can help you tune into your inner child and can help you experience the world with a sense of wonder and curiosity, just like a child.

Embracing your emotions is also crucial. As adults, we often suppress our emotions, but children express their feelings freely. So, allow yourself to feel joy, sadness, anger, and fear without judgment. This can help you reconnect with your inner child.

Lastly, take care of your inner child. This means treating yourself with kindness and compassion, just like you would treat a child. This can involve self-care activities like taking a bath, reading a book, or taking a nap. By taking care of your inner child, you can cultivate a sense of inner peace and happiness.

What Are The Steps to Embracing Your Inner Child?

Remember, reconnecting with your inner child is a journey, not a destination. It takes time and patience, but the rewards are well worth it. By embracing your inner child, you can unlock a sense of joy and happiness that can enrich your adult life.

Mindfulness and Meditation Practices

Practicing mindfulness is another effective way to reconnect with your inner child. Children are naturally present in the moment, not worrying about the past or the future. By practicing mindfulness, you can tap into this childlike state of being, helping you to enjoy the present moment more fully.

Mindfulness and meditation are practices that can greatly contribute to embracing your inner child, and subsequently, to adult happiness. Mindfulness involves being fully present in the moment, aware of your surroundings, thoughts, and feelings without judgment. This practice can help you reconnect with the simple joys and wonder that children often experience in their daily lives.

Meditation, on the other hand, is a practice where an individual uses a technique – such as mindfulness, or focusing their mind on a particular object, thought, or activity – to train attention and awareness, and achieve a mentally clear and emotionally calm and stable state. It can help you to quiet the noise of daily life and focus on your inner self, including your inner child.

Embracing your inner child through mindfulness and meditation can involve practices such as mindful play, where you engage in activities you enjoyed as a child but with a mindful approach. This could be coloring, playing a game, or simply observing nature. The goal is to immerse yourself in the activity, experiencing it fully without letting your mind wander to other concerns or judgments.

Another practice could be meditative visualization, where you imagine yourself as a child, recalling the feelings and experiences of that time. This can help you reconnect with that part of yourself, and bring those positive feelings into your adult life.

Mindfulness and meditation are not only about focusing on the positive. They also involve acknowledging and accepting the full range of your experiences and emotions, including those associated with your inner child. This acceptance can lead to greater self-understanding and self-compassion, key components of adult happiness.

It's important to note that mindfulness and meditation are skills that require practice. It's normal to find them challenging at first, but with time and consistency, they can become a valuable part of your routine, helping you to embrace your inner child and unlock greater joy in your adult life.

Research has shown that these practices can have numerous benefits for mental health. They can reduce stress, improve concentration, increase self-awareness, and promote emotional health. By helping to cultivate a more peaceful, accepting state of mind, they can create the conditions for the inner child to emerge.

Fascinatingly, this percentage demonstrates the significant impact that integrating elements of our childhood selves into our adult lives can have. Much of the joy derived from embracing the inner child appears to stem from placing a priority on laughter, joy, and curiosity—the qualities most commonly associated with youth. Furthermore, regularly tapping into this less inhibited, more spontaneous aspect of ourselves encourages a deeper sense of authenticity and self-acceptance.

Essentially, embracing your inner child is not merely a nostalgic trip down memory lane but a path toward self-awareness and emotional well-being. Additionally, it is not an overnight transformation but a gradual process that demands sensitivity, patience, and understanding—a journey worth embarking upon for its potential to transform one's perspective on life, enhancing happiness and holistic well-being.

Mindfulness, in general, is a type of meditation where you focus on being intensely aware of what you're sensing and feeling in the moment, without interpretation or judgment. Practicing mindfulness involves breathing methods, guided imagery, and other practices to relax the body and mind and help reduce stress.

In the context of embracing your inner child for a happier adult life, mindfulness can be particularly beneficial. It allows you to reconnect with the simple joy and pleasure of play, something that children often experience but adults tend to overlook.

How Do I Channel My Inner Child through Meditation and Mindfulness?

Activities and Exercises to Awaken Child-like Joy

Engaging in creative activities is one way to connect with your inner child. This could involve painting, drawing, or even building with Lego blocks. These activities not only foster creativity, but they also provide an outlet for self-expression and can help to reduce stress.

Typically, play is associated with childhood because it is during these formative years that we embrace play as a primary mode of expression and learning. However, incorporating elements of play into our adult lives should not be overlooked or underrated. Dr. Stuart Brown, a leading expert in the study of play, paints a clear picture of its significance: "Play is not just essential for kids; it can be an important source of relaxation and stimulation for adults as well."

Perhaps you recall the last time you really lost yourself in an engaging activity—maybe while painting, playing a musical instrument, or participating in a sport. This state of immersive engagement, also known as flow, is a perfect example of play in adulthood. Psychologists have found that experiences of flow can lead to improvement in confidence, motivation, and concentration.

You might stop and wonder how it is possible to incorporate play into a busy adult routine. Can it coexist with the demands and responsibilities that accompany adulthood? The answer is an unequivocal yes. It may involve prioritizing play, making it a non-negotiable element in your day. For some, it could mean incorporating short bursts of play into the day, like making a game out of everyday tasks. Others may dedicate specific times for recreational play, like weekend games or regular evening hobbies.

To truly embrace your inner child, it is crucial that you acknowledge the role of play in both your emotional well-being and cognitive function. Rediscover the games and activities that brought you joy, and make conscious efforts to include them in your routine. Give yourself permission to relish the joys of playful activities without feeling guilty. In the process, you are bound to reconnect with your inner child, boost your mental health, and enhance overall life satisfaction.

Adding an element of play to your time spent in nature can also be instrumental in embracing your inner child. Consider engaging in activities that you enjoyed as a child such as jumping in puddles, exploring a forest, beachcombing, or flying a kite. These actions can incite pure, uninhibited joy, akin to what a child would experience.

Research backs up these practices, affirming an undeniable link between time spent in nature and reduced stress, anxiety, and depression. Expressing creativity also nurtures the inner child, and nature provides abundant inspiration. You could try open-air painting, photography, or even crafting with found objects. The point is not to create a masterpiece, but to connect with the joy and freedom that children find in creativity.

Another practical step to nurture your inner child is swap screen time for green time. With technological encroachment into our lives, reconnecting with nature can be a profound counterbalance that allows us to tap into our childlike curiosity. The wonders of nature, from watching a bird build its nest, observing a caterpillar transform into a butterfly, or even just touching the rough bark of a tree, can spark a sense of marvel that makes lucid our connection with our inner child.

Storytelling is another activity that can help to connect with your inner child. This could involve reading a favorite childhood book, watching a beloved childhood movie, or even telling your own stories. Storytelling allows us to tap into our imagination and can help to foster a sense of wonder and curiosity.

Reading children's books or watching children's movies can also help you to connect with your inner child. These forms of media often contain themes of hope, wonder, and magic that can help to rekindle your sense of innocence and joy.

For example, Disney, a household name synonymous with fairytales and joyous childhood memories, is not only popular among children but also significantly influential for adults. The phenomenon of adult Disney enthusiasts may be viewed as an embodiment of tapping into one's 'inner child'. This innate innocence and curiosity, often perceived as an artifact of youth, is nonetheless an integral part of our adult selves. As per psychologists, maintaining a healthy relationship with this 'inner child' could contribute significantly towards fostering adult happiness and mental well-being.

Undeniably, the concept of the 'inner child' may initially seem complex to grasp. It is not a throwback to childhood phases or an excuse for immature behaviors. Instead, it refers to your primal, instinctual responses and dormant creativity that gets often overshadowed by adult responsibilities. Embracing your 'inner child' is a journey of unlearning to learn – discarding protective barriers of adulthood, and allowing oneself to be inquisitive and emotionally expressive.

This process requires an understanding of your authentic emotions, acceptance of your childhood experiences, and a willingness to address your unfulfilled needs. Doing so can reap emotional rewards, yielding greater happiness, stress management, and enhancing overall life satisfaction. Likewise, incorporating a degree of child-like joy and wonder into everyday adult life does not mean shirking responsibilities or ignoring the realities of adulthood. Rather, it is about finding balance—allowing oneself to experience simple pleasures, to remain curious, and to engage with the world with openness and enthusiasm. This delicate balance encourages psychological resilience and fosters greater empathy towards oneself and others. Indeed, embracing your inner child could be one of the most rewarding journeys you undertake for yourself.

Understanding this concept is crucial to grasp why such elements draw out our childlike enthusiasm. The term 'inner child' refers to an individual's childlike aspect, including everything from the capacity to enjoy innocent fun to the ability to feel and express honest emotions. It's a part of our psyche that encompasses emotions, creativity, spontaneity, and vulnerability usually associated with our childhood.

Cultivating a healthy relationship with your inner child could pave the way to a joyful and more fulfilled adult life. It's about reconnecting with the passionate, creative, and vibrant spirit of our younger selves before life shaped us into reserved adults. By acknowledging and nurturing our inner child, we can integrate these qualities into our adult lives, thereby fostering happiness and contentment.

In essence, the popularity of Disney among adults could be seen as a manifestation of this idea. It's a testament to the enduring relevance of the inner child to our well-being, a beacon calling us to reconnect with the enthusiasm, innocence, and curious spirit we once embraced free of inhibition.

"Growing old is mandatory, but growing up is optional."

- Walt Disney

Engaging in a dialogue with your inner child can reveal significant insights about your emotions, behaviors, and triggers. This process encourages you to revisit your early experiences, viewing them from your current reality, and in doing so, providing your inner child with much-needed empathy and reassurance.

Journaling or letter writing opens the door to a personal sanctuary within us, where past wounds can be healed, and self-growth can be fostered. It also surfaces emotions that might have been suppressed, providing a safe space to express those feelings and work through them.

Consider beginning your journal entry or letter with a gentle acknowledgment of your inner child, an affirmation of your acceptance, or a promise to listen. There's no singular correct approach to journaling to your inner child, so don't overthink the process. Instead, allow it to flow naturally, and remember that the journey towards embracing your inner child is a uniquely personal one that mirrors your individual path toward overall happiness.

Remember, the goal of these activities is not to act childish, but rather to reconnect with the joy, curiosity, and creativity of our childhood.

By embracing our inner child, we can lead happier, more fulfilled adult lives. As you proceed, allow yourself to delve deep into the emotions and memories that resurface, and take the time to understand them from your current standpoint. The ultimate goal is self-understanding, self-acceptance, and self-love.

"We don't stop playing because we grow old; we grow old because we stop playing."

- George Bernard Shaw

Chapter 6

Playfulness and Creativity

Encouraging Play and Creativity in Daily Life

By incorporating elements of playfulness and creativity in our everyday existence, one channels a crucial part of accepting your inner child and nourishing happiness in adulthood. The notion of play is not exclusive to the realm of children; it equally serves as a calming and invigorating outlet for adults. It paves the pathway for expressing oneself, sparking innovation, and embarking on journeys of exploration, each of which are crucial ingredients for leading a balanced and fulfilling existence.

Play can take many forms in adult life. It could be as simple as doodling on a notepad, playing a game, or engaging in a hobby. The key is to find activities that are enjoyable, and engaging, and allow for a break from the routine and pressures of adult responsibilities. These activities should be seen not as frivolous but as essential components of a balanced life.

Creativity, like play, is not confined to any age group. It is a powerful tool for self-expression and problem-solving. Encouraging creativity in daily life can involve activities such as writing, painting, cooking, or even coming up with new ways to solve everyday problems. Creativity stimulates the mind, provides a sense of accomplishment, and can lead to increased happiness.

In endorsing your inner child via the vehicles of play and creativity, it's vital to grant oneself the freedom to err and glean lessons from the mishaps. This mindset champions a sense of exploration and development, as opposed to harboring a fear of failure. It's a matter of savoring the journey as much as the destination and discovering happiness and gratification in the true essence of creation.

Ultimately, endorsing the essence of play and innovation in your day-to-day routine necessitates dedication and allocation of time and space for these endeavors. This might involve reserving specific periods for 'play' or 'creativity', or incorporating these joyful and inventive methods into your usual responsibilities.

Prioritizing fun and play is crucial for embracing your inner child and enhancing adult happiness. Fun and play are not just for children; they are essential elements for adults too. They help in reducing stress, boosting creativity, improving relationships, and promoting overall well-being.

Fun and play allow us to experience joy, excitement, and a sense of spontaneity, which are often lost in the hustle and bustle of adult life. They enable us to live in the moment, appreciate our surroundings, and engage fully with life. This can lead to a more profound sense of satisfaction and happiness.

Play also fosters creativity and innovation. When we allow ourselves to engage in playful activities, we open our minds to new possibilities and perspectives. This can enhance problem-solving skills, promote adaptability, and stimulate intellectual growth.

Engaging in fun and play can also improve our relationships. Shared moments of joy and laughter can strengthen bonds, promote empathy, and foster a sense of belonging and community. This can lead to improved social connections, which are vital for our emotional health and happiness.

Moreover, fun and play can contribute to our physical health. They often involve physical activities that can improve cardiovascular health, boost the immune system, and promote overall physical well-being. This can lead to increased energy levels, improved mood, and enhanced quality of life.

As for creativity, it is a fundamental aspect of human life that offers numerous benefits. One of the most significant is its role in problem-solving. Creative thinking allows us to approach problems from different angles, often leading to innovative solutions that traditional, linear thinking may not uncover.

Creativity also enhances our personal growth and self-understanding. Through creative activities, we can express our thoughts, feelings, and experiences, often leading to greater self-awareness and emotional health. This can be particularly beneficial for those dealing with stress or trauma, as creative expression provides a safe outlet for difficult emotions.

Moreover, creativity can contribute to improved mental health. Engaging in creative activities can serve as a form of meditation, helping to calm the mind and reduce anxiety. It can also boost mood and provide a sense of accomplishment, which can be particularly beneficial for those struggling with depression or low self-esteem.

Creativity can also foster social connections. Whether it's through collaborative projects, sharing creative work, or simply discussing creative ideas, these interactions can lead to deeper relationships and a sense of community. This can improve our overall happiness and well-being.

Furthermore, creativity can lead to increased job satisfaction. Many employers value creative thinking, as it can lead to innovative ideas and solutions. Being able to express creativity at work can make tasks more enjoyable and fulfilling, leading to greater job satisfaction.

Practicing creativity in daily life can also help in maintaining cognitive health as we age. Creative activities like painting, writing, or playing an instrument can keep the mind active and engaged, potentially delaying the onset of cognitive decline.

In conclusion, creativity offers a myriad of benefits, from improved problem-solving and self-understanding to enhanced mental health and social connections.

"The creative adult is the child who has survived."

- Ursula K. Le Guin

Workshops and Creative Exercises

In your journey to reconnect with your inner child, consider integrating workshops and creative exercises into your daily routine. Unlike conventional practices which may primarily emphasize logical and critical thinking, these activities prioritize the creativity and imagination inherent within your inner child.

Participating in workshops or committing to individual activities that foster creativity is an effective strategy. These can be artistic endeavors such as painting, storytelling or dance, but they're by no means limited to the arts. Anything that allows you to freely express your feelings and ideas from cooking a new recipe to arranging a bouquet of flowers–can serve to awaken the slumbering child within.

Many adult education centers and community programs offer workshops designed to stimulate creativity in a supportive, non-judgmental environment. These settings provide an opportunity for play and exploration, encouraging you to take risks and make mistakes – just like a child. As research in the field indicates, such environments enable adults to recapture the vitality and optimism of childhood, contributing significantly to their well-being and happiness.

Furthermore, regular practice of creative exercises at home can serve to nurture your inner child. These exercises might include free writing, sketching, collaging, or any other activity that sparks joy and encourages free expression. Remember, the goal here is not to create a masterpiece but to simply enjoy the process of creation. Allow yourself the freedom to make mistakes and experiment, for it's in these moments the inner child finds its voice.

Honoring your inner child through workshops and creative exercises is a journey of rediscovery. It's about reclaiming the openness, curiosity, and playful engagement that often become lost in adulthood. It's about finding the innocence of self-expression that doesn't fear judgment. So, venture forth, unhindered by the constraints of adult life, and foster the imagination that lies within your inner child.

Are You Nurturing Your Inner Child's Creativity?

Take this Quiz!

1. When was the last time you engaged in a creative activity just for fun?

- Within the last week
- Within the last month
- Within the last year
- Can't remember/I never do it

2. How often do you allow yourself unstructured time to explore new ideas?

- Frequently, it's part of my routine
- Sometimes
- Rarely
- Never

3. How often do you incorporate elements of play into your day?

- Every day
- Once a week
- Once a month

- Never

4. How willing are you to try new things without fear of judgment?

- Very willing

- Somewhat willing

- Not very willing

- Never willing

If your answers gravitate more towards the "Can't remember" or "Never," you could indulge in your creative inner child more! See below for some ideas:

How to Foster a Deeper Connection with Your Inner Child's Creativity:

- Unstructured play: Dabble in activities that don't have a determined final outcome, offering the freedom to create and experiment. It could be as simple as building with blocks or doodling on paper.

- Engage in artistic activities: Take on activities such as painting, pottery, writing, or even cooking. Being hands-on stimulates memory and imagination, encourages self-expression, and pulls you away from the realities of adulthood towards more childlike wonder.

- Learn something new: Take up a course or a hobby that you've always wanted to try but never had the time for. The learning process excites the brain, pushes boundaries and inspires creativity.

- Immersive environments: Surround yourself with art, music, nature or movies. These experiences can evoke emotions, inspiration and new perspectives, all of which contribute to a creative mind.

- Explore and wander: Travel, whether it's to a new city or just the other side of town. Meeting new people and observing new environments can stimulate curiosity and broaden the horizons of the mind.

- Revisit childhood: Reminisce by revisiting your old hobbies, watching your favorite childhood movies, or reading your favorite children's books. This can reignite emotions and ideas from when you were young and most creative.

By inviting your inner child to play and express itself in these ways, you pave the way for a more creative, happier, and fulfilled self.

Success Stories

Delving into the experiences of individuals who have embodied their inner child within their therapeutic practices, we witness compelling evidence of the transformative role this has played in their professional success and personal fulfillment.

One such case is Dr. Paula Jackson Jones, a renowned psychotherapist. After a few years into her practice, she began incorporating inner child therapy, reported experiencing numerous benefits, most significantly, heightened creativity and improved connections with her patients. The playful and spontaneous mindset allowed her to establish a better rapport with her clients and offer unconventional solutions. Her ability to embrace the inner child's traits bolstered her practice and was instrumental in her receiving the prestigious Psychology Pioneer Award.

On the other hand, Dr. Kurt Rathmann, a successful clinical psychologist, has embraced his inner child by incorporating its principles into his daily routines. His adoption of a playful mindset and an open heart to new possibilities allowed him to see therapeutic problems from fresh perspectives, propelling his successful intervention strategies. Placing utmost importance on allowing unstructured time for himself to explore new ideas, he encourages his patients also to do the same. Dr. Rathmann's therapeutic success can be largely attributed to his dedication to nurturing his inner child, which has greatly influenced his work in the field of psychology.

It's not just in a therapeutic context that these professionals have reaped the benefits of embracing their inner child. Apart from experiencing professional growth, both Dr. Jones and Dr. Rathmann spoke extensively about their personal improvements in overall mood, life satisfaction, and emotional well-being. They avow that by allowing room for their inner child to breathe, they have found more happiness and balance in their personal lives.

These success stories underscore the immense potential benefits of embracing and nurturing your inner child, not only for your professional growth but also for your personal life.

Cultivating a relationship with this inner child can be crucial to our emotional health, self-understanding, and overall happiness as adults. On a fundamental level, embracing your inner child means being open to the wonder, innocence, and joy that was a part of your younger self.

It also means acknowledging the pains, traumas, and fears that were a part of your early years.

Connecting with your inner child allows you to rediscover your inherent curiosity and zest for life, which often gets buried in the hustle and bustle of adult life. This may form an essential part of personal growth, creativity, and emotional intelligence. It invites fun, creativity, and spontaneity back into your life, which over time can enhance your overall well-being and restore a balance that often gets lost in responsibility and routine.

Interestingly, it was found that people who maintain a playful disposition throughout life are more likely to experience lower levels of stress, better physical health, and increased happiness. Research led by the National Institutes of Health sheds light on the importance of maintaining a playful disposition, illustrating that it can lead to substantial enhancements in mental and physical health. By embracing your inner child, you enable yourself to tap into a source of stress relief that many people de-prioritize as adults.

Indeed, incorporating elements of play into your lifestyle can contribute towards notable improvements in your well-being. For example, engaging in activities that spark joy and encourage creativity can promote resilience, and problem-solving skills, and facilitate emotional healing. These benefits highlight why it's essential to reintegrate play into your life—fostering a relationship with your inner child promotes relaxation, reduces anxiety, and creates a sense of inner peace, making it an essential component of adult happiness.

Furthermore, research suggests that when individuals allow themselves to explore new ideas and experiences without fear of judgment, they cultivate a more robust sense of self-acceptance and self-expression. Incorporating unstructured 'play' time into your daily routine can keep your mind nimble and responsive—stimulating creativity, and brain function, and contributing to overall life satisfaction.

So, whether it's through art, music, physical activities, or merely giving oneself permission to daydream—pursuing these activities for the simple joy they bring, without focusing on outcome or performance, can unlock the door to a more joyful, balanced life. Embrace your inner child, and you will undoubtedly see a transformation in your overall perspective and quality of life.

In conclusion, the key to tapping into the numerous benefits of honoring your inner child centers around engaging in play and creative activities, embracing novel experiences and ideas, and creating room in your life for unstructured exploration. A sense of intrinsic motivation, or doing things mainly for your own satisfaction rather than some external reward, plays a crucial role in promoting creativity and happiness.

Nurturing and embracing the child within isn't about living in the past or shying away from adult responsibilities; instead, it's about merging the wisdom of being an adult with the playfulness and imagination of being a child. By integrating these seemingly disparate aspects, one can attain a balanced sense of self and experience fulfillment on a deep level.

Ask Yourself: Are You Fostering Your Inner Child on a Daily Basis?

1. How regularly do you acknowledge and validate your feelings, much like how you would do for a child?

2. When was the last time you spent a few quiet moments with yourself, just enjoying your own company?

3. Do you give yourself the permission to fail and learn, rather than always pushing for perfection?

4. How often do you let your curiosity lead the way, exploring without knowing what you'll find?

5. Do you allow yourself guilt-free indulgence in things that simply bring you joy?

6. How much of your day is spent on activities that genuinely nourish your soul?

As you continue your introspective journey, remember to periodically take stock of your progress. Are you indulging in leisurely activities that make your heart dance in joy? Are you opening up to new experiences and ideas without fear of judgment? At the end of the day, the measure of success lies in being true to yourself and making space for the child within to express freely and boldly.

Remember, it's never too late to tend to the needs of your inner child, to heal old wounds, and to discover the joy of living with an open heart. Feel inspired to explore, create and experience the world anew through the eyes of your inner child. Swing back the doors of perception, and invite the unique gifts of imagination, spontaneity, and resilience your inner child brings into play. After all, the adult you are today is the child you were yesterday, still alive and eager to make every moment count.

Chapter 7

Emotional Healing

Addressing Past Traumas and Healing Wounds

Emotional healing is a critical process that involves addressing past traumas and healing wounds to unlock joy and embrace your inner child. It's about acknowledging and understanding the emotional pain and distress that past experiences may have caused and working towards resolving these issues to achieve a healthier and happier adult life.

Past traumas can significantly impact an individual's emotional health and overall well-being. These traumas, often experienced during childhood, can lead to emotional wounds that persist into adulthood if not properly addressed. They can influence how we perceive ourselves, how we interact with others, and how we respond to various situations. They can also lead to a variety of mental health issues, such as anxiety, depression, and post-traumatic stress disorder (PTSD).

Embracing your inner child is an integral part of emotional healing. The inner child represents the innocence, joy, and naturalness that we all had as children but may have lost touch with as we grew into adults. By reconnecting with this part of ourselves, we can regain the ability to experience pure joy, creativity, and spontaneity.

Embracing your inner child involves acknowledging and accepting all aspects of your childhood experiences, both positive and negative. It's about giving yourself permission to feel and express emotions freely, just like a child would. This can help you heal from past traumas and emotional wounds, as it allows you to process and release pent-up emotions.

By addressing past traumas and healing emotional wounds, you can unlock joy and embrace your inner child for a happier adult life.

PTSD and The Inner Child

Post-traumatic stress disorder (PTSD) is a mental health condition that's triggered by a terrifying event, either experiencing it or witnessing it. Symptoms may include flashbacks, nightmares, severe anxiety, and uncontrollable thoughts about the event. The concept of the 'inner child' refers to an individual's childlike aspect, including what a person learned subconsciously and absorbed from their parents and environment during childhood.

PTSD and the inner child are interconnected in the sense that traumatic experiences from childhood can significantly impact an individual's adult life, often manifesting as PTSD. This is because the child within us holds onto those traumatic experiences, leading to a variety of emotional, psychological, and behavioral issues in adulthood.

The complex dynamics between PTSD and the inner child aren't linear but multi-faceted. The childlike part that resides within each adult has an inherent capability of resilience and adaptation. However, this does not negate the fact that the wounds of past traumas can silence this inner child, making them retreat into a metaphorical hiding spot deep within the psyche.

Yet, understanding these dynamics is crucial to facilitating healing and fostering a sense of inner peace. Being aware and sympathetic towards one's inner child can guide adults in exploring and confronting the lasting effects of childhood trauma.

For instance, psychotherapy, particularly trauma-informed therapy, plays a pivotal role in this process. Renowned trauma therapist and author Dr. Bessel van der Kolk shares his insights on this intriguing interplay between PTSD and the inner child: "Often, adults with PTSD are subconsciously living through the lens of a frightened child. Therapy helps them confront this perspective, unveiling paths towards healing and reassurance." This highlights the importance of therapeutic engagement, addressing inner child wounds to effectively encourage growth and healing from past traumas.

Trauma-informed therapy works by helping individuals safely revisit their past traumas, hereby shedding light on their impacts and helping to articulate feelings that have long been suppressed or mislabeled. You may initially experience reluctance or fear when facing these past traumas. However, it's essential to remember that it's a step towards reclaiming your happiness and control over your life.

Experts suggest envisioning oneself as offering comfort and safety to their inner child. This therapeutic strategy can eventually help the affected individual develop a sense of self-compassion, healing old wounds and gradually liberating the silenced inner child.

In conclusion, your inner child, even when deeply affected by traumatic experiences, is a beacon of hope, a testament to resilience, and an intrinsic part of who you are. Embracing them is the first step toward understanding yourself better, letting go of the past, and paving the way to an emotionally healthier future.

Therapeutic Methods for Inner Child Work

Whether you're struggling with anything from PTSD to a disconnection with your inner child, there are many options for professional help and therapy. Healing these emotional wounds involves recognizing the trauma, understanding its impact, and taking steps toward recovery.

This process often requires professional help, such as therapy or counseling. Therapists can provide various techniques and strategies, such as cognitive-behavioral therapy (CBT), eye movement desensitization and reprocessing (EMDR), and trauma-focused cognitive behavioral therapy (TF-CBT), to help individuals cope with their traumas and heal their emotional wounds. See the table below for more information.

Types of Inner Child Therapy Work

Consider this hypothetical case: Take Emily, a 40-year-old female who has been living with unexplained anxiety, flashbacks, and nightmares for years. Since childhood, Emily experienced trauma due to physical abuse from her parents. These traumatic experiences resulted in suppressed emotions and damaged her inner child, causing PTSD.

Emily sought therapy and was advised Cognitive-Behavioral Therapy (CBT), Eye Movement Desensitization and Reprocessing (EMDR), and Trauma-focused Cognitive Behavioral Therapy (TF-CBT). Initially, she underwent CBT, which helped her understand that her distressing physical and emotional responses were due to her traumatic past and not current circumstances. It also aided in reducing negative thought patterns that perpetuated her anxiety.

Next, Emily was subjected to EMDR, which had her recall the traumatic experiences while receiving bilateral stimulation–usually eye movements. This method worked at 'reprogramming' the memory of the traumatic events, allowing for the resolution of emotional distress.

TF-CBT was the final therapy utilized, primarily because it was designed to assist children and adolescents with post-traumatic symptoms. Although Emily is an adult, her psychological distress stems from traumatic events in her childhood–thus, her healing needs to include the restoration of her inner child. Procedures in this therapy helped Emily process her traumatic memories, manage distressing feelings, and enhance safety, growth, parenting skills, and family communication.

The whole process of therapy aimed to heal her wounded inner child and empower her adult self with more resilience. After several months of therapy, Emily reported substantial improvement in her symptoms, displaying better-coping mechanisms and a considerably improved quality of life. The healing of Emily's inner child was key to her successful recovery from PTSD. As she dealt with her childhood traumas, she simultaneously freed her adult self from living in constant fear and anxiety.

This case underlines the importance of recognizing and caring for the inner child in adults with PTSD. In many cases, the inner child holds the scars of past trauma, and addressing these injuries can be a crucial factor in achieving overall mental wellness.

Inner Child Testimonials: Jessica and Martin

The healing power of reconnecting with your inner child is not merely a theoretical concept; rather, it is a reality that many have experienced firsthand. There are multiple real-life stories of individuals who have found solace, comfort, understanding, and indeed healing, by reintroducing themselves to their inner child. Jessica's Journey to Self-realization

Consider Jessica's narrative, for example, a woman who was mired in clinical depression and anxiety for several years. But when she started working on her inner child, she experienced a notable shift in her life. She rediscovered the joy she knew as a child and began to view the world through a much more optimistic lens. "I journaled, painted, played like I did in my childhood, and gradually, I could see my anxiety receding. It felt as if my inner child was teaching my adult self how to live again," Jessica shared.

Similarly, Martin, a man who was living with the burden of past traumatic events, found respite and healing by embracing his inner child. "Some of my earliest memories are filled with fear and loneliness. They were like shadows, subtly influencing my adult life. As I began to connect with my inner child, I also started confronting these shadows. Instead of feeling fear, I was filled with an understanding that these were just memories," recounts Martin. He further explained how embracing his inner child became a transformative experience, helping him to 'rewrite' his traumatic past in a healthy way.

For both Jessica and Martin, healing came about by acknowledging and addressing the needs of their inner child. They express that the process helped them to approach life not as wounded adults, but as empowered individuals, capable of growing and healing from past hurts.

These stories underscore the significance and implications of embracing your inner child. There may be laughter, and there may be tears, but ultimately, as demonstrated by both Jessica and Martin, there is an opportunity for profound healing and rejuvenation.

Chapter 8

Overcoming Resistance

Dealing With the Fear of Judgment and Self-doubt

Fear of judgment and self-doubt are common obstacles that can hinder our ability to embrace our inner child and experience joy. These fears often stem from past experiences and societal expectations. It's crucial to understand that everyone has their own unique journey and that it's okay to be different.

Self-doubt is often a result of internalizing negative feedback or criticism. It's important to remember that everyone makes mistakes and it's through these mistakes that we learn and grow. Instead of viewing mistakes as failures, view them as opportunities for growth and learning. This shift in perspective can help alleviate self-doubt.

Dealing with the fear of judgment requires developing resilience and self-confidence. This can be achieved by focusing on your strengths and accomplishments. Celebrate your wins, no matter how small they may seem. This will help build your self-esteem and reduce the fear of judgment.

Another effective strategy is practicing self-compassion. This involves treating yourself with the same kindness and understanding you would offer to a good friend. When you make a mistake or face a setback, instead of criticizing yourself, respond with kindness and understanding.

Additionally, it can be helpful to surround yourself with positive influences. Seek out supportive friends, family, or mentors who encourage and uplift you. Their positive feedback can help counteract negative self-perceptions and reduce fear of judgment.

Remember, embracing your inner child is about letting go of societal expectations and embracing your authentic self. By dealing with fear of judgment and self-doubt, you can unlock joy and lead a happier adult life.

Indeed, managing judgment, be it self-imposed or coming from others, is integral not only to embracing your inner child but ultimately to leading a fulfilled emotionally healthy life. Here are some strategies that may aid you in this process:

Strategies For Managing Judgment and Self-doubt

- Acknowledge your feelings: The first step towards handling judgment is to acknowledge your feelings. Do not suppress or deny the emotions that arise. Recognize them and thus validate your own experience.

- Unhook from criticism: Understanding that criticism is an opinion and not an objective fact can be a critical shift in perception. Do not perceive criticism as a personal attack, but rather view it as feedback that you can choose to accept or reject.

- Practice self-compassion: Understand that everyone is susceptible to error, and flawed experiences do not define your worth. Rather than berating yourself for perceived shortcomings, practice forgiveness and approach your missteps with understanding and patience.

- Reframe your interlocutor's perspective: Observing the judgmental comments with empathy, and considering the possibilities of conflicts, fears, or insecurities that may prompt the person to pass judgments can be therapeutic and help reduce the impact on you.

- Develop a supportive network: Surround yourself with positive, constructive individuals who respect and appreciate you for who you are. Their support can act as a buffer against the negativity and judgment of others.

- Embrace self-affirmation: Positive affirmations help to reinforce your self-esteem and reduce the damage from harmful judgments. Make it a habit of talking positively about yourself and affirming your self-worth.

- Seek professional help: If judgments are causing significant distress, it may be beneficial to seek the guidance of professionals such as therapists or counselors who can provide specialist tools and strategies for managing them.

In conclusion, remember that the power to handle judgment from others begins with you. The more kindly you can treat yourself, the less hurtful the assault from societal judgments will be.

The path to overcoming these internal and external barriers begins with acceptance. Recognizing and wholeheartedly accepting your inner child is crucial. It may involve revisiting past memories, both pleasant and painful. Try to see the world again from your child-self's perspective. This requires courage and resilience, but with practice, it becomes a powerful tool for self-healing and growth.

Accepting your inner child is fundamentally about acknowledging and accepting this often-neglected aspect of your personality. Your child-like self forms an essential part of who you are, influencing your decisions, thoughts, behaviors, and emotional responses. Acceptance of the inner child may not be a straightforward process given its possible connection to painful childhood memories. Yet, it serves as an enlightening journey toward self-awareness and personal growth.

Acceptance of your inner child encompasses various layers of introspection. On one level, acknowledging the existence of your inner child entails peering into the mirror of your past. It means coming to terms with the unique experiences that shaped your childhood. On another level, it signifies listening compassionately to the needs and wants of your inner child. These may be needs for safety, attention, or love, which may have been unmet in the past. Fundamentally, it involves showing kindness and compassion to your inner self, much like a parent would to their child.

As you progressively grow more accepting of your inner child, you infuse your adult life with a renewed sense of vigor and dynamism. It propagates a more authentic lifestyle as you connect with your deeper passions and instincts. Most importantly, inner child acceptance brings forth abundant joy and happiness, hailing the manifestation of authentic well-being.

Acceptance, thus, lies at the core of fostering companionship with your inner child. By willingly delving into the depths of your psyche, you learn to cultivate a nurturing relationship with your innermost self. Welcoming your resident child-self into the arena of your adult life liberates you from unresolved conflicts and unfulfilled needs.

Steps to Accepting the Inner Child

1. Embrace your emotions: You were once that child who felt fear, joy, anger, and sadness. Accepting these feelings as valid and normal parts of the human experience helps to form a bond with your inner child. Working towards emotional intelligence and literacy allows you to better communicate with that part of yourself.

2. Practice Self-Care: Promote reconnection with your inner child by tending to its needs for rest, nutrition, and fun. Engaging in activities you once loved or found enjoyable is a great way to rekindle that connection.

3. Create a Safe Space: Create an environment where it's safe to explore, play, and make mistakes. This reinforces the concept that it's okay to be vulnerable and not have all the answers—a mindset intrinsic to childhood.

4. Express Yourself Creatively: This can take the form of drawing, painting, writing, or any other form of uncensored expressive activity.

Such activities allow your inner child to communicate and solidify its identity within you.

5. Be patient: Acceptance does not happen overnight. It's a process involving patience and persistence. Periods of regression are natural and part of the journey towards self-acceptance. The key is being consistent and gentle with your inner child.

6. Seek Professional Guidance: Therapists and counselors trained in inner child therapy can offer strategies and tools for embracing and healing this fundamental aspect of your psychological makeup. They provide insightful assistance and guidance in unlocking past traumas and nurturing your inner child.

Encouragement and Advice from Experts

From leading psychologists and neuroscientists, a wealth of wisdom has been accumulated on the matter of embracing your inner child. One of the most prevalent insights among these experts is the necessity of allowing yourself to access the emotional landscape of your formative years. By recalling and accepting the experiences that shaped you, you afford yourself a deeper understanding of your personality and your emotional triggers. You can intentionally revisit these experiences, not to indulge in the past, but to acknowledge them as a part of your journey to who you are.

The aforementioned Dr. Lucia Capacchione, a pioneer in the field of creative journaling and inner child work, urges, "Don't try to analyze or judge your inner child, rather, approach them with patience, kindness, and a willingness to learn."[1] It's important to remember that the inner child is not just a concept or a symbolic figure—they are a real part of you, one that harbors your primal emotions and most intimate feelings.

This vibrant, yet often neglected entity within you engulfs spontaneous joy, unbridled curiosity, dynamic creativity, and a profound sense of awe. It embodies your capacity for innocence, wonder, and excitement. Yet, it can also be a repository for deep-seated traumas, unexpressed emotions, and buried memories.

Adopting a welcoming attitude towards your inner child implies opening a dialogue with this part of yourself. Dr. Eric Berne[2] (1910 – 1970), a Canadian-born psychologist and founder of Transactional Analysis Theory, suggested engaging in 'child ego state' conversations. In these dialogues, you lead as the 'adult ego state', interacting with your inner child in a loving, understanding, and non-judgmental manner.

Postulated in the 1950s, his Transactional Analysis Theory fundamentally altered the way the field understood interpersonal communication. This revolutionary principle centers on the idea of 'ego states'. See the table below for more information.

Berne's theory underscores the importance of each of these states in maintaining a balanced and emotionally healthy personality. It is, however, the 'child ego state' that forms the core of our current discussion. By encouraging adults to tap into this realm, Berne has paved the way to exploring avenues for embracing our innate emotional selves, thereby activating profound avenues for self-awareness and personal growth.

If this communicative process seems challenging, consider enlisting the help of a trained professional. Therapists specialized in inner child work provide the necessary guidance to facilitate healing dialogues and foster inner child connection. They use a range of therapeutic techniques such as guided imagery, expressive arts, and play therapy which incorporate the non-verbal communication favored by the child's ego state.

One poignant example of this therapeutic process involved a 35-year-old client named Sarah. Sarah approached the therapist, troubled by the perpetual feeling of worthlessness that had pervaded her adult life despite her significant achievements. Her therapist recognized this as an indication of unresolved issues relating to her inner child, resulting from a difficult childhood characterized by emotional neglect.

The therapy sessions were designed to help Sarah bridge the gap with her inner child. They began with guided imagery, which helped Sarah visualize the way her insecurity originated from her unhealed inner child. The therapist encouraged her to construct a safe space within her imagination where she could meet and talk with her younger self.

Gradually, through expressive arts and play therapy, Sarah started communicating non-verbally with her inner child, engaging her in joyful activities that she missed during her actual childhood. She painted pictures, acted out scenarios, and even sang songs that allowed her to express feelings and experiences she was unable to verbalize.

With each session, Sarah felt progressively connected to her inner child. She developed empathy for her younger self, nurturing a healthy dialogue that allowed her inner child to express fears and anxieties. This empathetic encounter reaffirmed her self-worth, diminishing the feelings of worthlessness that dominated her adult life.

This therapeutic journey indicates how trained professionals can form a bridge between adults and their inner child, providing the necessary communion that leads to self-healing. Through a combination of guided imagery, expressive arts, and play therapy, therapists are able to facilitate communication pathways that forge a nurturing alliance with the unhealed child within.

Chapter 9

Integrating the Inner Child in Adult Life

Balancing Adult Responsibilities With the Needs of the Inner Child

Balancing adult responsibilities with the needs of the inner child involves a delicate interplay of acknowledging both aspects of oneself. The inner child represents our most authentic self, the source of our joy, creativity, and curiosity. However, as adults, we also have responsibilities and tasks that require maturity and practicality.

Firstly, it's important to recognize and validate the existence of your inner child. This can be done through self-reflection, meditation, or therapy. Acknowledging your inner child allows you to understand its needs and desires, which often include play, creativity, and emotional expression. This understanding can help you incorporate these needs into your adult life.

Secondly, create a safe space for your inner child to express itself. This could be through art, music, dance, or any other form of creative expression that you enjoy. Allowing your inner child to play and create can bring a sense of joy and fulfillment that can counterbalance the stress of adult responsibilities.

Thirdly, practice self-care and self-love. The inner child often carries emotional wounds from childhood that need healing. By practicing self-care, you can provide the nurturing environment necessary for this healing process. This can also help you manage stress and maintain a healthy balance between your adult responsibilities and the needs of your inner child.

"Our inner child is still a child. He or she needs to be nurtured."

- Thich Nhat Hanh

Lastly, it's crucial to set boundaries. While it's important to embrace your inner child, it's equally important to not let it take over completely. There are times when adult responsibilities must take precedence. Setting boundaries helps maintain a healthy balance between the needs of your inner child and your adult responsibilities.

Balancing the needs of your inner child with your adult responsibilities is not a one-time task, but a continuous process. It requires self-awareness, patience, and a lot of self-love. But by doing so, you can unlock a level of joy and fulfillment that can greatly enhance your quality of life.

How Can Practicing Self-love Nurture My Inner Child?

1. Self-kindness: Instead of being overly critical or hard on oneself, embrace self-kindness. It entails treating oneself with the same care and concern that one would show to a dear friend or loved one under the same circumstances.

2. Common humanity: Recognize that everyone makes mistakes and suffers at times. Understanding this brings about a sense of belonging, helping you view your experience as part of the larger human experience and not something isolating or individual.

3. Mindfulness: This involves maintaining a balanced perspective and not suppressing or exaggerating feelings. It's about being fully present and consciously aware of our emotions, acknowledging them without judgment or endeavoring to immediately change them.

Cultivating a joyful relationship with your inner child is a significant part of embracing self-love. Remember, this inner child is essentially the emotional part of you, carrying your ability to experience surprise, joy, and innocence. Spending quality time with your inner child, therefore, rekindles these precious emotions that often get buried under the weight of adult responsibilities.

It might seem perplexing initially–how does one spend time with their inner child? Well, it's more straightforward than you might think. It can be as simple as engaging in activities you enjoyed as a child. This could include coloring books, playing with toys, exploring nature, or even watching your favorite childhood shows. These activities act as a conduit to your past, igniting emotions associated with simpler times.

Imagine a scenario where you're blowing bubbles in a park. In this moment, your focus shifts from your everyday stresses to the colorful, floating spheres. The very act brings a feeling of light-heartedness, an emotion often associated with childhood. The bubbles don't carry the weight of judgment or cynicism; they simply exist and bring joy. This moment encapsulates being present and embracing the simplicity of childhood joy.

Connecting to your inner child can also be an exploration of your past. Looking through old photo albums, reminiscing about past accomplishments or challenges, and acknowledging the child who endured and thrived can foster a loving bond with your inner child.

Case Studies

The journey of nurturing one's inner child can be illumination through the prism of real-life experiences. Let us take a closer look at two striking examples:

Case Study One: Sasha and the Brush Strokes of Joy

Sasha, a 45-year-old banker, lived a hectic, high-stress life focused solely on meeting deadlines and targets. One day, she stumbled upon a painting class for adults seeking to reconnect with their inner child. Intrigued, Sasha decided to step back from her demanding routine and immerse herself in this childhood activity. She began to allow her inner child to paint not just on canvas, but also on the tableau of her existence. After attending several classes, she started experiencing a profound sense of contentment and enjoyment in her daily life. By embracing her inner child, Sasha found happiness through creativity, a feeling she had disconnected from in her pursuit of career ambitions.

Case Study Two: Dave and the Beat of Innocence

For Dave, a successful lawyer in his mid-fifties, life was devoid of joy outside the courtroom triumphs. While attending a reunion, Dave heard old buddies reminiscing about their childhood drumming exploits. This conversation enlightened Dave about the existence of his suppressed inner child, leading him on a quest to reclaim the passion he once held for music. He soon purchased a drum set and started to rekindle the rhythm of his inner child. Dancing to this newfound beat, he discovered happiness in the echoes of his innocent past. Dave's story highlights how following the resonances of our inner child's interests can pave the way for adult happiness.

Therefore, the experiences of Sasha and Dave provide practical insights into how one can foster their inner child leading to a fulfilled and happier life. They exemplify that reconnecting with your inner child's desires and passions can unearth an untapped reservoir of joy and contentment in adulthood. Embracing one's inner child is not an escape from adult responsibilities, but rather an essential part of maintaining balanced mental well-being. So, isn't it time to listen to your inner child's whispers?

Advice on Maintaining this Balance Long-term

Maintaining a long-term balance between embracing your inner child and functioning as an adult requires consistent effort. Statistics affirm the relevance of fostering your inner child for adult happiness. According to a study conducted by the American Journal of Play, approximately 75% of adults who regularly engage in playful activities such as arts and crafts, sports, or games, reported feeling happier, more energetic, and less stressed. These individuals also demonstrated significantly improved productivity and creativity at work, implying a strong correlation between embracing one's inner child and overall life satisfaction.

Furthermore, a survey carried out by the Happiness Research Institute revealed that adults who foster their inner child saw an upswing of 30% in their contentment and satisfaction with life. They also reported a 20% reduction in stress levels and frustrations related to their day-to-day experiences, further substantiating the need to balance adult responsibilities with playful, child-like activities.

However, this balance is not easily achieved. A separate study conducted by the British Quality of Life Survey indicated that only around 42% of adults feel they have managed to consistently incorporate playful activities into their lives that truly allow their inner child to thrive.

These statistics highlight the crucial role the inner child plays in adult life and underscore the benefits of investing in more joyful and child-focused activities. Accepting and nurturing your inner child is not just a fanciful theory; its importance is evidenced by tangible and statistically significant benefits.

One of the most effective ways to achieve this is by integrating play into your daily routine. This doesn't necessarily mean playing with toys or games, but rather engaging in activities that bring you joy and allow you to express your creativity. This could be anything from painting to dancing, hiking, or even cooking a new recipe.

Another crucial aspect of maintaining this balance is practicing mindfulness. Being present in the moment allows you to fully experience your emotions, both positive and negative. This can help you connect with your inner child, as children tend to live in the present rather than worrying about the past or future. Mindfulness can be cultivated through practices such as meditation, yoga, or simply taking a few moments each day to focus on your breath and surroundings.

Self-care is also essential in maintaining this balance. This includes taking care of your physical health through regular exercise and a balanced diet, but also your mental and emotional health. Make sure to set aside time for relaxation and activities that you enjoy. It's also important to seek professional help if you're struggling with mental health issues.

Communication is another key factor. Expressing your feelings and needs honestly and openly can help you maintain a healthy relationship with your inner child. This can be done through journaling, talking to a trusted friend or family member, or seeking therapy. Remember, it's okay to ask for help when you need it.

Equilibrium in all aspects of one's life is foundational to nurturing your inner child. The quest for balance presumes the necessity of understanding the multidimensional nature of our lives, which includes work, family, friends, and oneself. Focusing excessively on one aspect while neglecting others may hinder growth and create disconnection with your inner child.

Balancing work and personal life, a topic often discussed is critical in this regard. In the busyness of today's world, it can be difficult to carve out space for self-reflection and rest. You must make an effort to schedule "me time," whether that be pursuing a hobby, reading a book, or going for a walk in nature. This gives you the space to reconnect with your inner child and stimulates a more balanced frame of mind.

Striking a balance within your relationships is also an important aspect to consider. Interactions with friends and family provide a sense of belonging and security which can comfort and heal your inner child. However, it's equally important to communicate your boundaries effectively. Ensuring others respect your personal space helps maintain a healthy emotional environment where your inner child can thrive.

Similarly, maintaining a sense of balance in your physical health can significantly impact your mental and emotional state. Regular exercise, a balanced diet, and sufficient sleep are fundamental elements of overall well-being. It's essential not to overlook these points as they can profoundly affect your inner child's happiness.

On a final note, it's worth considering that your pursuit of balance shouldn't become a source of stress in itself. Accept that some days will be more balanced than others, and give yourself the grace to be imperfect. After all, your inner child values the process and the love you bring to it, more than any perfectly balanced day.

Striking a harmonious balance between all aspects of your life can allow your inner child to flourish. Here are some methods to consider:

- Setting Boundaries: Sometimes, the key to balance is learning when to say 'no'. Establishing clear, healthy boundaries can help preserve your emotional well-being and free up time for self-care and enjoyable interests.

- Prioritizing Time for Yourself: Just as you would schedule a meeting at work or a doctor's appointment, it's crucial to block out time purely for your own enjoyment or relaxation. This could be as simple as a quiet moment with a book, or a larger commitment like a weekly fitness class.

- Maintaining Connections: Relationships with loved ones are a vital part of living a balanced life. Such connections can provide emotional support, shared experiences, and a sense of belonging.

- Nurturing Healthy Habits: Regular exercise, a nourishing diet, and adequate sleep are cornerstones of a physically balanced lifestyle. Accordingly, these habits can significantly bolster your emotional health.

- Being Present: Cultivate mindfulness, which means being fully engaged in the current moment. It can assist you in reducing stress and appreciating the smaller wonders in everyday life.

- Embracing Flexibility: Acknowledge that balance doesn't mean being perfect or keeping every area of your life in equal proportion all the time. Some days you may need to devote extra attention to one area, and that's okay.

In conclusion, developing these practices can be a pathway toward a more balanced life. The journey may require patience and adaptation, but gradually you will notice how this practice enriches not only your life but also enhances your connection to your inner child.

Chapter 10

Relationships and the Inner Child

The Inner Child and Adult Relationships

Connecting with your inner child can significantly improve relationships by fostering empathy. The inner child represents our most authentic self, full of innocence and curiosity. By reconnecting with this part of ourselves, we can better understand our own emotional needs and reactions, which in turn allows us to empathize more deeply with others. This heightened empathy can lead to more meaningful and satisfying relationships.

Tuning into your inner child can also help in resolving conflicts. Often, our reactions to conflicts are shaped by past experiences and unresolved childhood issues. By acknowledging and addressing these issues, we can respond to conflicts in a more mature and constructive manner. This can lead to healthier communication and less friction in our relationships.

Another benefit of connecting with your inner child is the ability to bring joy and spontaneity into relationships. The inner child is associated with playfulness and creativity. By allowing this aspect of ourselves to shine, we can infuse our relationships with more fun and excitement, keeping them vibrant and dynamic.

Moreover, embracing your inner child can help in setting healthy boundaries in relationships. The inner child is often associated with our needs and desires. By understanding and honoring these needs, we can communicate our boundaries more effectively. This can lead to more balanced and respectful relationships.

Lastly, connecting with your inner child can foster self-love and acceptance. The process of embracing your inner child often involves healing old wounds and forgiving past mistakes. This can lead to a stronger sense of self-worth, which is a key factor in building healthy and fulfilling relationships.

What Are the Benefits of Practicing Self-love?

Communication Skills and Emotional Intelligence Development

Communication skills and emotional intelligence are two key elements that play a significant role in embracing your inner child and fostering adult happiness. Communication skills are not just about speaking and listening, but also about understanding and interpreting the emotions, needs, and desires that underlie the words we use.

Emotional intelligence, on the other hand, is the ability to understand, use, and manage your own emotions in positive ways to relieve stress, communicate effectively, empathize with others, overcome challenges, and defuse conflict. It also involves your perception of others: when you understand how they feel, this allows you to manage relationships more effectively.

The linkage between emotional intelligence and the concept of the inner child is a complex yet fascinating aspect of psychology. Emotional intelligence, as your ability to identify, comprehend, and constructively utilize your emotions, extends to an understanding of the emotions of others as well. Recognizing and nurturing your inner child essentially taps into this dimension of emotional intelligence.

The inner child represents the deeply imprinted aspects of our childhood experiences, the unfiltered expression of emotions, desires, and creativity. It's the central ethos of our purest emotions, holding our capacity for genuine joy, curiosity, and love. However, often it also encompasses our deepest fears, insecurities, and pains that we experienced during our formative years.

Emotional intelligence is indispensable in addressing the needs of the inner child. Harnessing emotional intelligence for your inner child allows you to tap into these raw, often neglected emotions. This connection allows individuals to manage and express feelings in a healthy manner, addressing and healing childhood wounds that may be creating obstacles in their current lives.

In essence, high emotional intelligence gives the means to recognize your inner child's needs, identify unattended emotional injury, and then use those insights to foster self-understanding and personal growth. When we allow ourselves to tenderly revisit, and then fundamentally tap into that innocent, uninhibited version of ourselves, we open ourselves up symbolically to a whole new world of empathy, understanding, and healing.

Moreover, navigating your relationships, be it personal or professional, involves understanding the emotional dynamics at play. As you nurture your inner child under the light of emotional intelligence, you become more adept at empathizing with others and managing relationships.

What Are the Benefits of Practicing Good Communication?

Developing these skills starts with self-awareness. This involves recognizing your own emotions and how they affect your thoughts and behavior, understanding your strengths and weaknesses, and having self-confidence. It's about paying attention to your emotional state and identifying your emotional triggers.

Social awareness is also crucial. This involves understanding the emotions, needs, and concerns of other people, picking up on emotional cues, feeling comfortable socially, and recognizing the power dynamics in a group or organization.

In the end, relationship management is key. This involves knowing how to develop and maintain good relationships, communicate clearly, inspire and influence others, work well in a team, and manage conflict. All these skills contribute to unlocking joy and embracing your inner child for a happier adult life.

Testimonials

Ample instances present themselves where couples and families have reaped rewards from their efforts to nurture their inner child, leading to improved relationships. Let's review a few enlightening examples.

The dynamic of Kathy and Robert, a couple undergoing relationship tension, is a classic example of the transformation that results from embracing the inner child. Initially, their communication was plagued with misunderstandings and intense arguments. However, turning to a different path, they decided to foster their inner child's presence. Recalling innocent joy and a carefree spirit in their interactions, they began to tackle difficult conversations with a touch of playfulness. They started incorporating humor and light-heartedness into their talks, which miraculously resolved their frequent misunderstandings. Their relationship improved significantly, showcasing the potent impact of the inner child.

Similarly, the story of the Johnson family stands testament to the power of the inner child in transforming family relationships. Narwhal-like, they appeared to be swimming in an ocean of discord, with members of the household blame-shifting and living disconnected lives despite sharing the same roof. Their son's school counselor suggested they explore the realm of the inner child as a means of building stronger connections. Intrigued by the concept, they started engaging in childlike activities together such as board games, picnics, and playful competitions. This shift from their normal pattern sparked dialogue and laughter amongst the family members, fostering a palpable sense of unity. The Johnsons now enjoy a robustly connected familial relationship, one that they credit to their exploration and acceptance of their inner children.

These stories serve as proof that acknowledging and cherishing the inner child can manifest in profound improvements in relationships. Whether within couples or families, reforging bonds with the innocence and playfulness inherent in the concept of the inner child, can facilitate communication, enhance understanding, and foster a deeper sense of interconnectedness.

When we delve deep into the realm of statistics surrounding the revitalizing effect of embracing the inner child in therapy, the data are indeed, quite illustrative. According to a widely cited study conducted in 2012 by Clinical Psychology and Psychotherapy Journal, therapy focusing on one's inner child resulted in notable progress in 74% of the relationships studied. Patients reported enriched connections, improved understanding, and heightened empathy in their relationships.

Further, another significant study by the Journal of Marital and Family Therapy in 2015 evaluated the impact of 'inner child-focused therapy' on couples. The impressive results revealed an average improvement in marital satisfaction ratings of 75%, with the reported increase in emotional intimacy as the likely primary driver.

Moreover, a survey conducted in 2018 by the American Psychological Association brought to light the wider benefits this approach can yield in family relationships. They reported that in approximately 63% of families, greater emotional bonding and stronger ties emerged from energetically embracing the child within. The study further found signs of improved parental understanding and reduced conflicts in families.

In conclusion, these statistics provide compelling evidence of the power of inner child therapy in enhancing emotional bonding, understanding, and overall satisfaction in various types of relationships. The data is undeniable: honoring the inner child can have significant positive effects on interpersonal connections.

Chapter 11

The Inner Child at Work

Bringing Joy and Creativity into the Workplace

Fostering the inner child in the workplace can lead to a more joyful and creative environment. This concept is based on the psychological theory that our inner child, the part of us that remains innocent, spontaneous, and curious, can be a source of great joy and creativity. By tapping into this aspect of ourselves, we can bring a sense of playfulness and innovation to our work.

Creating a workplace that encourages playfulness can lead to increased creativity. This doesn't mean turning the office into a playground, but rather fostering an environment where ideas can be freely expressed, where mistakes are seen as opportunities for learning, and where curiosity is encouraged. This can be achieved through team-building activities, brainstorming sessions, and providing spaces for relaxation and informal conversations.

Encouraging employees to embrace their inner child can also lead to greater job satisfaction and happiness. When people feel free to express themselves and approach their work with a sense of playfulness, they are likely to be more engaged and motivated. This can lead to increased productivity, better team dynamics, and a more positive workplace culture.

However, it's important to strike a balance. While embracing the inner child can bring many benefits, it's also crucial to maintain professionalism and respect for others. This means creating a safe and inclusive environment where everyone feels valued and heard.

Embracing the inner child in the workplace is not just about creating a happier and more creative environment, but also about promoting mental health. By allowing space for playfulness and self-expression, we can help reduce stress and burnout, leading to a healthier and more productive workforce.

How Can Embracing Your Inner Child Improve Your Work Performance?

- Innovation: Embracing the inner child encourages spontaneity and creativity, key aspects that drive innovation. By encouraging employees to tap into their childlike sense of exploration, businesses can foster a culture of innovation and problem-solving.

- Adaptability: Children are naturally adaptable, constantly learning and adjusting to new situations. Encouraging employees to connect with their inner child can improve their adaptability in the face of change and uncertainty.

- Motivation: The tendency of children to see things in a new and exciting light can be brought into the professional environment. This fresh perspective can reactivate the passion and motivation in employees, pushing them to perform at their best.

- Collaboration: Children tend to work well in groups and are open to cooperation. Invoking the child within can improve teamwork and collaboration, resulting in a more unified, synergistic workforce.

- Resilience: Children are often resilient, bouncing back from failure quickly and without dwelling on negative outcomes. Promoting a connection with the inner child can enhance employees' resilience, improving their capacity to recover from setbacks and keep striving for success.

- Energy: Children abound with energy and enthusiasm. By embracing the inner child in the workplace, businesses can stimulate a more energetic and dynamic work environment.

Interviews with Leaders

Exploring the mindset of innovative leaders and entrepreneurs provides valuable insight into the importance of embracing one's inner child for enhanced work performance.

Renowned CEO, Melissa Goldberg emphasized that staying in touch with my inner child allows me to approach challenges creatively and uniquely. She further illustrated that by maintaining the openness and curiosity of her childlike mind, she can perceive unconventional paths towards problem-solving in her business, a trait frequently absent in the austere corporate world.

Gary Roberts, a leading entrepreneur, shared similar sentiments, My inner child is a continual source of motivation and tenacity. It helps me persist through the trials that inevitably arise in an entrepreneurial journey. The raw determination we often associate with our younger selves aids me in overcoming these obstacles.

Janice Gordon, an accomplished innovation consultant, expanded on the therapeutic benefits of embracing your inner child, stating that regularly engaging with my playful, light-hearted side acts as a form of self-care. It allows me to maintain a balanced sense of well-being amidst a high-pressure job.

These interviews collectively highlight the significance of securing a relationship with your inner child. Not only does it foster novel ways of thinking and persistent determination, but also serves as a means of self-care and maintaining emotional balance. The input from these leaders underscores how embracing and nurturing your inner child can catalyze personal and professional growth.

You might wonder, "How precisely can this bond with my inner child enhance my personal and professional development?" Let's delve into this deeper. Psychology experts posit that this connection can stimulate elements of your personality that often lay dormant, such as curiosity, creativity, and adaptability. These are not only attributes of a highly functional adult but also core characteristics of progressive professionals.

Your inner child recalls a time when you were more willing to explore and recognize the unfamiliar without any fear. Invoking this nostalgia can reignite your creativity, driving you to seek inventive solutions and ideas eagerly. This fosters a powerful and innovative work environment, one where out-of-the-box ideas are not only encouraged but propagated.

The relationship with your inner child also helps to develop resilience. Remember the determined child who repeatedly fell off the bike but continued to get back on until they mastered riding without a hitch? That tenacity tends to diminish under the weight of adult responsibilities. However, by reconnecting with that determined child within, you can revive the resilience and grit necessary to face professional challenges and roadblocks head-on.

"Do not erase the designs the child makes in the soft wax of his inner life."

- Maria Montessori

Furthermore, nurturing your inner child has profound implications for self-care and emotional well-being. An active and acknowledged inner child equips you with better emotional regulation, leading to greater emotional intelligence (EQ). A high EQ is invaluable in the workplace, fostering empathetic communication, better teamwork, and more strategic leadership.

Finally, in a world where change is the only constant, adaptability becomes an essential tool. The unburdened joy and flexibility of a child, their willingness to adjust, adapt, and enjoy new circumstances can be a helpful reminder of how to deal with change as an adult.

In conclusion, building a genuine connection with your inner child equips you with critical tools and skills that have far-reaching benefits personally and professionally. Embracing your inner child is not about eschewing responsibility or maturity. Instead, it's a way of integrating these crucial elements that contribute to a comprehensive, balanced state of being.

"In every real man a child is hidden that wants to play."

- Friedrich Nietzsche

Tips for Fostering a Playful and Productive Work Environment

Creating an environment where your inner child feels acknowledged and accepted can drastically improve your quality of work and overall productivity. Here are some suggestions for fostering this environment:

- Maintain a Positive Attitude: While it might seem simple, maintaining a positive attitude is key in forging a playful work environment. Positivity inspires creativity, boosts morale, and ignites the spirit of playfulness that connects us to our inner child.

- Change Your Scenery: The physical space in which we work has a significant impact on our productivity and ability to channel our inner child. Including elements of nature, such as plants or natural light, or adding vibrant colors that stimulate creativity can encourage a more energetic and youthful vibe.

- Encourage Breaks: Scheduling regular intervals for 'playtime' during the workday can help reduce stress and re-energize the mind. A quick game of ping-pong, doodling, or even walking around the block can reactivate the fun-loving kid within us and lend a fresh perspective to our work.

- Promote Collaboration and Open Communication: The spirit of a child thrives in an atmosphere of cooperation and clear communication. Encourage open dialogue and team projects where everyone's input is valued. Fostering a climate where innovative ideas are rewarded can bridge the gap between work and play.

- Incorporate Fun into Learning: Learning doesn't have to be monotonous or strictly formal. Incorporate fun elements into trainings and workshops, like interactive sessions, games, and team-building activities. This helps embrace the curious, learning-oriented nature of our inner child.

Many adults have found great success in their careers by embracing and channeling their inner child. Numerous professions thrive on the childlike qualities of curiosity and imagination. For instance, inventors and researchers continuously question the world around them and imagine new possibilities, much like children do.

Indeed, if we look closely at some of the most successful individuals within the spheres of invention, entrepreneurship, and innovation, it becomes apparent that their ability to tap into their inner child played a significant role. Remember, children view the world without the filters of preconceived ideas or societal norms that adults often possess. This perspective, which is simultaneously naive and profoundly intuitive, is the fertile ground from which fresh, ground-breaking ideas sprout.

Let's consider the example of Walt Disney, a titan of imaginative creativity. His extraordinary ability to harness the wonder, joy, and limitless imagination that is the hallmark of children allowed him to develop a multimedia empire whose influence continues to be felt to this day. Disney's famous quote speaks volumes: "That's the real trouble with the world. Too many people grow up." His success and legacy are a testament to the enduring value and relevance of the inner child within the adult realm.

"That's the real trouble with the world. Too many people grow up."

- Walt Disney

The key to leveraging your inner child for career success lies in balancing childlike qualities with adult responsibilities and pragmatism. Professionalism does not necessarily require you to suppress the child within you but to incorporate its wonder, imagination, and curiosity into your work.

To harness the power of your inner child, you may want to rekindle your youthful passions or hobbies. Revisiting these activities can unlock new ideas and perspectives that can be invaluable in your work. Additionally, fostering an open mindset, where you see every challenge or roadblock as an opportunity for growth and learning, can not only enrich your work but also bring a renewed sense of joy and fulfillment to your career.

When you allow your inner child to shine, you bring more authentic, creative, and joyful energy into your work, and these qualities can set you apart in your career. Embracing your inner child is not about being immature or irresponsible; rather, it's about infusing your work with the beautiful, positive characteristics of childhood that can lead to greater satisfaction and success in your career.

In conclusion, by integrating these principles into your work environment, you can create a playful, engaging atmosphere that nurtures your inner child and promotes happiness, creativity, and productivity.

Chapter 12

A Society Reconnected

Envisioning a World that Honors the Inner Child

The concept of the 'inner child' refers to an individual's childlike aspect, including everything they learned and experienced as children before puberty. Society plays a significant role in shaping this inner child, as it sets the norms, values, and expectations that we learn and internalize during our formative years.

Society often encourages us to suppress our inner child as we grow older, promoting maturity and responsibility over the spontaneity and curiosity typically associated with childhood. This suppression can lead to a disconnection from our authentic selves and potentially result in feelings of unhappiness or unfulfillment in adulthood.

Embracing the inner child in adulthood can be seen as a form of resistance against societal pressures to conform and 'grow up'. This doesn't mean shirking responsibilities or behaving immaturely, but rather allowing oneself to experience joy, wonder, and curiosity typically associated with childhood.

By acknowledging and nurturing our inner child, we can lead a more balanced life. It allows us to maintain our sense of playfulness and spontaneity, even as we navigate the complexities of adult life. This balance can contribute to overall happiness and satisfaction.

According to a study published in the Journal of Personality and Social Psychology, individuals who maintain a connection with their inner child can experience up to 15% more happiness compared to those who don't. This connection, which is defined in the study as the ability to engage in activities associated with childhood, such as playing games or daydreaming, is not only essential for boosting joy but can also reduce stress levels in adults by as much as 33%. This shows the power of embracing the inner child within us.

A survey conducted by the American Psychological Association also supports these findings. Upon studying the habits of 2,000 adults, they discovered that those who regularly allocate time for fun and playful activities exhibit lower levels of stress and higher levels of happiness. Over 60% of the adults who participated in this survey admitted that playfulness contributes greatly to their overall well-being.

Lastly, a research study from the Journal of Positive Psychology emphasizes the role of the inner child in fostering resilience and optimism. People who can tap into their inner child can increase their capacity to deal with life's challenges and improve their overall health. In fact, the study puts forward that individuals who nourish their inner child could experience a 50% increase in their ability to handle adversity and an increase of 42% in overall job satisfaction.

These statistics provide compelling evidence about the significant impact our inner child can have on our happiness, stress levels, resilience, and overall satisfaction with life when we embrace and nourish it.

In the end, society and the inner child have a complex, intertwined relationship. While societal norms can often suppress the inner child, embracing and nurturing this aspect of ourselves can lead to a more fulfilling and joyful adult life.

Initiatives and Movements Promoting Play and Creativity in Adults

In recent years, an increasing number of initiatives and movements have emerged that promote the concept of play and creativity in adulthood. These endeavors draw on various disciplines including but not limited to psychology, neuroscience, business, and education, acknowledging the profound impact of leisure activities on our overall well-being.

A comprehensive survey conducted by the National Institute of Play revealed that 80% of adults who indulge in playful activities regularly experience significantly lower levels of stress. Furthermore, this group demonstrated a remarkable 60% increase in productivity and innovation at their workplaces. Clearly, endorsing the 'inner child' is not merely an esoteric concept but holds tangible benefits for our professional and personal lives.

Simultaneously, a 2019 study by the Creativity Research Journal mentioned that workshops promoting 'creative play' in adults have multiplied by 300% over the last decade. These workshops focus on a variety of creative domains, such as painting, writing, drama, and dance, and are designed to facilitate self-expression, mental resilience, and nurturing our inner child.

The 'Maker Movement', a cultural trend that places value on an individual's ability to craft and create, boasts 135% growth in the past five years alone, as per the Pew Research Center. This movement encourages adults to reclaim their creativity and imagination by engaging in activities that entail building and designing.

The corporate world is also realizing the significance of play for adults. As per a report by the Association for Talent Development, nearly 45% of Fortune 500 companies have incorporated play-based elements into their training programs. This evidence shows an increasing recognition of the importance of play in fostering creativity, teamwork, and problem-solving abilities among adults.

In conclusion, it's heartening to see that today's society is slowly but acknowledging the importance of nurturing our inner child. As adults, we're beginning to understand and value the power of play and creativity for our holistic health and happiness.

As part of this awakening awareness, several initiatives encourage adults to access their inner child. These range from therapeutic methods to community-based activities and creative hobbies that foster self-expression.

How to Reconnect to Your Inner Child Through Community

Through these initiatives, adults can reconnect with their inner child, a source of spontaneity, creativity, and genuine happiness often muted by the demands of adult responsibility. As more individuals embark on these journeys, our society becomes more attuned to the integral role of the inner child in overall well-being.

The Inner Child and Community Building

Embracing the concept of the inner child is not just a personal journey, but it can also be a collective endeavor. A call to action for community building around this idea can involve several steps. First and foremost, create awareness about the concept of the inner child and its impact on adult happiness. This can be done through workshops, seminars, and online platforms, where experts in psychology and mental health can share insights and practical tips.

Next, establish support groups where individuals can share their experiences and challenges in embracing their inner child. These groups can serve as safe spaces for individuals to express their feelings and fears, and to learn from others who are on the same journey. They can also provide a sense of belonging and community, which can significantly enhance the process of embracing the inner child.

Organize activities that encourage adults to reconnect with their inner child. This could include art workshops, play sessions, storytelling events, and other activities that foster creativity and playfulness. These activities can help individuals to tap into their inner child and experience the joy and freedom that it brings.

Encourage community members to practice self-care and self-love, as these are crucial in nurturing the inner child. This can be promoted through wellness programs, mindfulness sessions, and resources on mental health. By taking care of their physical, emotional, and mental well-being, individuals can create a nurturing environment for their inner child to thrive.

This is why we, as a society, must advocate for policies and practices that support mental health and well-being in the community. This could involve lobbying for mental health services, promoting work-life balance, and creating environments that are conducive to mental health and happiness.

By creating a community that values and supports mental health, we can make it easier for individuals to embrace their inner child and experience greater happiness in their adult lives. This process can become a shared endeavor within community settings, following these structured steps:

- Create awareness about the inner child: Utilize workshops, seminars, and online platforms to spread knowledge about the inner child concept and its connection to adult happiness. Involve experts in psychology and mental health to share insights and practical tips.

- Establish support groups: Form groups where individuals can freely share their experiences and challenges related to their inner child. These groups can serve as safe spaces for expression, learning, and the cultivation of a sense of community.

- Organize nurturing activities: Host events such as art workshops, play sessions, and storytelling that encourage adults to reconnect with their inner child. Activities fostering creativity and playfulness can facilitate the rediscovery of the joy and freedom residing in one's inner child.

- Promote self-care and self-love: Encourage community members to prioritize their well-being, which can significantly nurture the inner child. Wellness programs, mindfulness sessions, and mental health resources can be instrumental in taking care of physical, emotional, and mental health.

- Advocate for mental health policies: Encourage practices that support mental health and well-being in the community. Lobby for mental health services, promote work-life balance and strive to create environments conducive to mental health and happiness.

Chapter 13

Conclusion
A Life Transformed

Embracing your inner child is not a mere whimsical notion; it's an essential step to achieving a greater version of ourselves. When we allow ourselves to connect with our inner child, we tap into a fountain of boundless energy, imagination, curiosity, and most importantly, self-love. Here's how this subliminal acquaintance could revolutionize your life.

The first dramatic change you'll notice is **the blossoming of creativity**. As children, we were all budding Picassos and Shakespeares; there was no limit to what our imaginations could conjure. Reconnecting with that uninhibited creativity allows for original, innovative thoughts and ideas to flourish, setting the stage for breakthroughs in personal and professional lives.

An undeniable benefit of embracing your inner child is the palpable **increase in resilience**. As we grow older, we often lose the childlike resilience that enabled us to bounce back from disappointments quickly. By revisiting those innate qualities, we rekindle the ability to face life's adversities with renewed determination and a positive outlook.

To navigate the complexities of interpersonal interactions, we often resort to masks and pretenses. However, reconnecting with your inner child can facilitate **honest and authentic relationships**. As children, we were sincere in our communications, expressing emotions without fear or hesitation. By channeling this authenticity, we're able to foster deeper, meaningful connections, thereby enriching our social lives.

Moreover, at the heart of the inner child, lies a wellspring of **joy and fun**. Amidst the humdrum routine of adult life, we tend to sideline joy as a non-priority. But, creating space for spontaneous fun can drastically enhance the quality of life, arming us with sufficient energy and motivation to tackle our responsibilities.

Lastly, bonding with your inner child can nurture a profound **sense of empathy**. The child within understands vulnerability, fear, and the need for comfort. Embracing these emotions can deepen our empathy towards ourselves and others, fostering a kinder, more compassionate world.

In conclusion, embracing your inner child is a bold step towards an enriched, joy-filled life. It's about giving yourself the freedom to dream, to laugh, to create, and to love with the unabashed vigor of a child–a unique journey of self-discovery that holds the promise of a lifetime of happiness.

The Journey of Reconnecting with Your Inner Child

Simply put, reaching out to your inner child is a brave journey of self-discovery, not a regression into infancy or a means of escaping adult responsibilities. It is about acknowledging the part of you that is creative, energetic, and vibrant. By cultivating an empathetic connection with your inner child, you are effectively inviting joy, creativity, and resilience into your everyday experiences.

Embracing the inner child helps you to live a life that genuinely reflects your core values and passions. It promotes a sense of authenticity and harmony, enabling you to engage more fully with the world around you. As adults, we often tend to sideline this youthful essence, not realizing its potential to invigorate our lives. By nurturing this inner energy, you empower yourself with new ways to deal with life situations with a more flexible attitude and an open mind.

Remember, kindling a relationship with your inner child is a path of liberation. It encourages us to express our real emotions without fear of judgment or criticism. It opens up avenues for personal growth and encourages the embracing of vulnerability as a strength rather than a weakness. Don't view your inner child as a liability, but instead, see it as an untapped source of creativity, enthusiasm, and optimism, which can be instrumental in catalyzing positive changes in your life.

Liberate your inner child and let it reclaim the happiness, spontaneity, and creativity that modern life often quells. This is not a call to irresponsibility or mindless play, but an invitation to experience life in all its richness and variety. Your inner child has been waiting. Don't keep it waiting any longer.

Baby Steps to Begin Reconnecting with Inner Child

Embarking on the journey of reconnecting with your inner child may seem overwhelming initially. However, by breaking down this process into manageable, baby steps, it becomes a feasible venture. Let's get started:

1. Identify your inner child's needs: Reflect on your childhood, recollect the activities you thoroughly enjoyed and activities you were deprived of. Understanding the needs of your inner child, such as validation, creativity, expression, and play, lays the foundation for this exploration journey.

2. Prioritize fun: Encourage yourself to occasionally prioritize fun over work. This could be scheduling a weekly craft session, or simply setting aside time to watch cartoons that you loved as a child.

3. Engage in creative hobbies: Dabble in creative outlets like painting, writing, woodworking, baking, or DIY projects, which allow for self-expression and a break from logical, rigid thinking.

4. Incorporate unstructured time: Allow yourself to have unstructured time where you can freely think, dream, and wonder, much like a child does. This may feel uncomfortable at first, but it's a vital aspect of embracing your inner child.

5. Be mindful of your inner dialogue: Notice how you talk to yourself. Is it warm and nurturing or harsh and critical? Be gentle with yourself, and try to respond to your own mistakes, shortcomings, and insecurities with kindness and understanding, as you would to a child.

6. Practice spontaneity: Organized schedules and predetermined plans are typical for adults, yet spontaneity is a significant component of a child's behavior. Try being spontaneous whenever possible, it might be a random road trip or trying a new cuisine.

7. Engage with nature: Children have a natural affinity towards nature. Plan regular nature outings to a nearby park, garden, or forest and allow yourself to connect with the natural world freely and imaginatively.

Remember, the journey back to your inner child is a personal one and there's no definitive roadmap. The above steps serve as a general guide, and your unique process will likely contain additional steps. Enjoy the journey, learning about yourself, and cultivating a deeper connection with your creativity along the way!

Chapter 14

Appendices

Resources for Further Reading and Exploration

Need further convincing on the merits of nurturing your inner child? Check these essential readings:

- "Playing for Happiness: Embracing Your Inner Child" by Dr. James Prochaska

- "The Essentiality of Play: Releasing the Inner Child" by Marianne Williamson

- "Creativity and the Inner Child: How Play Shapes the Adult" by Dr. Alice Miller

- "Embracing the Inner Child within the Workplace: The Effects on Productivity and Motivation" by Dr. Carl Rogers

Professional Organizations for Inner Child Work

Embracing your inner child could potentially offer a wealth of benefits, and many seek to incorporate this concept into their self-improvement efforts. That being said, there are several workshops, courses, and retreats available that aim to facilitate this process.

One of the highly recommended tools is certified workshops from the Association for Play Therapy. This organization offers a range of resources, including certified workshops designed to help adults rekindle their playful spirit and unlock their creative prowess.

You might also consider online courses such as the "Healing Your Inner Child" course offered by Udemy. This comprehensive course provides lessons on understanding and nurturing your inner child, allowing for personal growth and emotional healing.

Retreats such as the Inner Child Healing Retreat held by Omandaway integrate therapeutic modalities, like yoga and meditation, with inner child work. These retreats provide a tranquil and supportive environment where you can delve deep into self-exploration and healing.

Each of these options offers unique approaches to embracing your inner child. Whether you choose a workshop, an online course, or a retreat, the most important thing is that you select a method that resonates with you personally. Investing in one of these opportunities not only facilitates personal growth and development, but it can also lead to increased happiness, satisfaction, and the ability to form deeper connections with others.

Types of Workshops

There exists a number of professional organizations that can provide guidance and assistance for individuals on a mission to nurture and embrace their inner child. Selecting the right organization can heavily depend on personal preference and specific needs, so conduct thorough research before making a decision.

One organization to consider is the Association for Play Therapy (APT). APT focuses not only on therapeutic work with children but also emphasizes the importance of the inner child in adults. They offer a range of resources, workshops, and certification programs for individuals looking to explore their own inner child or professionals in the field of psychology and therapy.

Another viable option is the International Expressive Arts Therapy Association (IEATA). They provide resources and advocacy for the use of creative expression as a tool for healing, aligning well with the concept of unlocking one's inner child through creativity and play.

Finally, the American Art Therapy Association (AATA) might also be of interest. Similar to IEATA, AATA focuses on harnessing the power of art to enhance psychological wellness. This can be a valuable resource for those seeking to nurture their inner child through creativity.

All of these organizations provide robust resources, educational materials, and networking opportunities. They are worth looking into for anyone seeking a more structured approach to embracing their inner child.

www.ingramcontent.com/pod-product-compliance
Lightning Source LLC
LaVergne TN
LVHW020447070526
838199LV00063B/4872